THE WAY
PEOPLE
LIVE

Life in a California Mission

Life in a California Mission

Titles in The Way People Live series include:

Cowboys in the Old West
Games of Ancient Rome
Life Aboard the Space Shuttle
Life Among the Great Plains Indians
Life Among the Ibo Women of Nigeria
Life Among the Pirates
Life Among the Samurai
Life Among the Vikings
Life During the American Revolution
Life During the Black Death
Life During the Crusades
Life During the Gold Rush
Life During the Great Depression
Life During the Middle Ages
Life During the Renaissance
Life During the Roaring Twenties
Life During the Russian Revolution
Life During the Spanish Inquisition
Life in a Japanese American Internment
    Camp
Life in a Medieval Castle
Life in a Medieval Monastery
Life in America During the 1960s
Life in an Amish Community
Life in a Nazi Concentration Camp
Life in Ancient Athens
Life in Ancient China
Life in Ancient Egypt
Life in Ancient Greece
Life in Ancient Rome

Life in a Wild West Show
Life in Berlin
Life in Charles Dickens's England
Life in Communist Russia
Life in Genghis Khan's Mongolia
Life in Hong Kong
Life in Moscow
Life in the Amazon Rain Forest
Life in the American Colonies
Life in the Australian Outback
Life in the Elizabethan Theater
Life in the Hitler Youth
Life in the North During the Civil War
Life in the South During the Civil War
Life in Tokyo
Life in War-Torn Bosnia
Life of a Medieval Knight
Life of a Nazi Soldier
Life of a Roman Slave
Life of a Roman Soldier
Life of a Slave on a Southern Plantation
Life on Alcatraz
Life on an African Slave Ship
Life on an Everest Expedition
Life on Ellis Island
Life on the American Frontier
Life on the Oregon Trail
Life on the Pony Express
Life on the Underground Railroad
Life Under the Jim Crow Laws

THE WAY
PEOPLE
LIVE

Life in a California Mission

by
Eileen Keremitsis

LUCENT
BOOKS®

THOMSON
———★———™
GALE

San Diego • Detroit • New York • San Francisco • Cleveland • New Haven, Conn. • Waterville, Maine • London • Munich

On cover: A friar prays in the garden
of a California Mission.

LIBRARY OF CONGRESS CATALOGING-IN-PUBLICATION DATA

Keremitsis, Eileen.
  Life in a California mission / by Eileen Keremitsis.
    p. cm. — (The way people live)
  Summary: Discusses the history of California missions, their dual purpose of converting
people to Catholicism and consolidating Spanish territory, and the daily life of friars,
natives, and soldiers.
    Includes bibliographical references (p.   ) and index.
    ISBN 1-59018-159-X (alk. paper)
   1. California—History—To 1846—Juvenile literature. 2. Missions, Spanish—
California—History—Junvenile literature. 3. California—Social life and customs—
18th century—Juvenile literature. 4. California—Social life and customs—19th century—
Juvenile literature. 5. Indians of North America—Missions—California—Juvenile
literature. 6. Franciscans—California—History—Juvenile literature. [1. California—
History—To 1846. 2. Missions—California—History. 3. California—Social life and
customs. 4. Indians of North America—Missions—California. 5. Spaniards—California—
History. 6. Frontier and pioneer life—California.] I. Title. II. Series.

  F864 .K37 2003
  979.4'02—dc21

2001008100

Contents

FOREWORD
    Discovering the Humanity in Us All   8

INTRODUCTION
    Spain in the Americas   10

CHAPTER ONE
    Founding the Missions   14

CHAPTER TWO
    The Making of a Missionary   25

CHAPTER THREE
    Recruiting Converts   37

CHAPTER FOUR
    Daily Life of the Mission Indians   49

CHAPTER FIVE
    Daily Life of the Friars   67

CHAPTER SIX
    Daily Life of the *Gente de Razón*   80

EPILOGUE
    Last Days of the Missions   93

    Notes   96
    For Further Reading   99
    Works Consulted   101
    Index   105
    Picture Credits   111
    About the Author   112

Discovering the Humanity in Us All

Books in The Way People Live series focus on groups of people in a wide variety of circumstances, settings, and time periods. Some books focus on different cultural groups, others, on people in a particular historical time period, while others cover people involved in a specific event. Each book emphasizes the daily routines, personal and historical struggles, and achievements of people from all walks of life.

To really understand any culture, it is necessary to strip the mind of the common notions we hold about groups of people. These stereotypes are the archenemies of learning. It does not even matter whether the stereotypes are positive or negative; they are confining and tight. Removing them is a challenge that's not easily met, as anyone who has ever tried it will admit. Ideas that do not fit into the templates we create are unwelcome visitors—ones we would prefer remain quietly in a corner or forgotten room.

The cowboy of the Old West is a good example of such confining roles. The cowboy was courageous, yet soft-spoken. His time (it is always a he, in our template) was spent alternatively saving a rancher's daughter from certain death on a runaway stagecoach, or shooting it out with rustlers. At times, of course, he was likely to get a little crazy in town after a trail drive, but for the most part, he was the epitome of inner strength. It is disconcerting to find out that the cowboy is human, even a bit childish. Can it really be true that cowboys would line up to help the cook on the trail drive grind coffee, just hoping he would give them a little stick of peppermint candy that came with the coffee shipment? The idea of tough cowboys vying with one another to help "Coosie" (as they called their cooks) for a bit of candy seems silly and out of place.

So is the vision of Eskimos playing video games and watching MTV, living in prefab housing in the Arctic. It just does not fit with what "Eskimo" means. We are far more comfortable with snow igloos and whale blubber, harpoons and kayaks.

Although the cultures dealt with in Lucent's The Way People Live series are often historically and socially well known, the emphasis is on the personal aspects of life. Groups of people, while unquestionably affected by their politics and their governmental structures, are more than those institutions. How do people in a particular time and place educate their children? What do they eat? And how do they build their houses? What kinds of work do they do? What kinds of games do they enjoy? The answers to these questions bring these cultures to life. People's lives are revealed in the particulars and only by knowing the particulars can we understand these cultures' will to survive and their moments of weakness and greatness.

This is not to say that understanding politics does not help to understand a culture. There is no question that the Warsaw ghetto, for example, was a culture that was brought about by the politics and social ideas of Adolf

Hitler and the Third Reich. But the Jews who were crowded together in the ghetto cannot be understood by the Reich's politics. Their life was a day-to-day battle for existence, and the creativity and methods they used to prolong their lives is a vital story of human perseverance that would be denied by focusing only on the institutions of Hitler's Germany. Knowing that children as young as five or six outwitted Nazi guards on a daily basis, that Jewish policemen helped the Germans control the ghetto, that children attended secret schools in the ghetto and even earned diplomas—these are the things that reveal the fabric of life, that can inspire, intrigue, and amaze.

Books in The Way People Live series allow both the casual reader and the student to see humans as victims, heroes, and onlookers. And although humans act in ways that can fill us with feelings of sorrow and revulsion, it is important to remember that "hero," "predator," and "victim" are dangerous terms. Heaping undue pity or praise on people reduces them to objects, and strips them of their humanity.

Seeing the Jews of Warsaw only as victims is to deny their humanity. Seeing them only as they appear in surviving photos, staring at the camera with infinite sadness, is limiting, both to them and to those who want to understand them. To an object of pity the only appropriate response becomes "Those poor creatures!" and that reduces both the quality of their struggle and the depth of their despair. No one is served by such two-dimensional views of people and their cultures.

With this in mind, The Way People Live series strives to flesh out the traditional, two-dimensional views of people in various cultures and historical circumstances. Using a wide variety of primary quotations—the words not only of the politicians and government leaders, but of the real people whose lives are being examined—each book in the series attempts to show an honest and complete picture of a culture removed from our own by time or space.

By examining cultures in this way, the reader will notice not only the glaring differences from his or her own culture, but also will be struck by the similarities. For indeed, people share common needs—warmth, good company, stability, and affirmation from others. Ultimately, seeing how people really live, or have lived, can only enrich our understanding of ourselves.

Spain in the Americas

The mission period began in California in 1769 with the founding of the mission in San Diego. The mission period lasted until the mid-1830s. During this time twenty-one missions were created from San Diego to north of San Francisco, over a distance of 650 miles.

The missions had two primary objectives: one was religious, the other political and territorial. As the high-ranking Spanish official, Visitor-General Don José de Gálvez, explained on the eve of founding California's first missions in 1768, "The object is to establish the Catholic Faith, to extend the Spanish domain, to check the ambitious schemes of a foreign nation."[1]

These two objectives grew from a sequence of events dating to Christopher Columbus's New World voyage of 1492. At that time the pope granted Spain rights to all of North and South America, except Brazil (which had already been claimed by Portugal). In return for these lands, Spain agreed to establish colonies and bring the indigenous peoples into the Christian fold.

Viceroyalty of New Spain

In order to administer such a large territory, the king of Spain created the post of viceroy, or second in command. The king separated his American empire into two administrative units, called viceroyalties. The capital of the South American viceroyalty was established in what became the city of Lima, Peru. The rest of the Spanish territory became the Viceroyalty of New Spain. New Spain reached from what is now Panama through Central and North America. Its capital was in Mexico City.

Over the years Spanish language, culture, and the Catholic religion spread throughout much of the colonies. However, distant regions, such as California, were largely overlooked.

Foreign Threats

California's relative isolation did not last. In the mid-1700s, foreign ships—including Russian otter hunters and New England whalers—had begun to show a great deal of interest in lands along the Pacific Ocean. This was the same land Spain had earlier claimed for itself. The Spanish king became concerned that he might lose control of his far-flung empire.

The king sent a special envoy to the colony of New Spain in 1765. He was charged with investigating ways of strengthening Spanish control there. This envoy, Visitor-General Don José de Gálvez, recommended establishing new Spanish settlements in the area then known as Alta California (today's California). Knowing it would be difficult to attract settlers to California, Gálvez proposed a solution that had worked earlier in northern Mexico, Baja California, and other parts of New Spain. His solution relied on a combi-

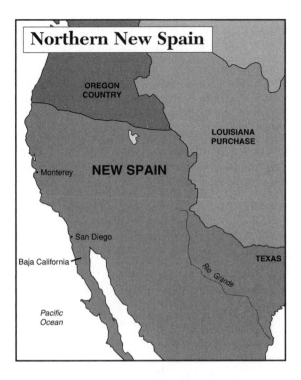

Northern New Spain

OREGON COUNTRY

LOUISIANA PURCHASE

NEW SPAIN

Monterey

San Diego

Baja California

TEXAS

Rio Grande

Pacific Ocean

cisco Bay in 1826, summarized the goals of the California missions when he wrote: "The object of the missions is to convert as many of the wild Indians as possible and to train them within the walls of the [mission] establishment in the exercise of a good life, and of some trade, so that they may in time be able to provide for themselves and become useful members of civilized society."[2]

A New Way of Life

By the end of the mission period, in the mid-1830s, life for California's indigenous population had changed dramatically. Before the first mission was founded, the coastal region of California was home to about one hundred thousand Indians, who lived much as their ancestors had lived for thousands of years. They used Stone Age types of tools to support themselves by fishing, hunting, and gathering wild seeds, grains, and nuts. Their dwellings were simple huts gathered into villages. From fifty to five hundred Indians lived in a village. Indians in one village might speak the same language as their neighbors, or they might speak one of the thirty or more mutually unintelligible languages used in California, where there were no major tribes or political systems.

In only sixty-five years of mission life in California, the economy and society of coastal California were transformed. Traditional ways of life, for the most part, disappeared. Some forty thousand Indians had converted to Catholicism, learned to speak Spanish, ride horses, and farm. (Many thousands more Indians had died, mostly from European diseases to which they had no resistance.) Along with a few dozen Franciscan missionaries, the native Californians had created farms and ranches that spread over vast

nation of presidios and missions. The presidios (military garrisons) and missions (communities of Indians led by Spanish friars) would be founded at strategic locations along the California coast. The presidios would provide military backup, but the real weight behind the Spanish claim to California would be in the mission population.

Mission Goals

For the Spanish, a mission was a place where Indians could be brought together, converted to Roman Catholicism, and taught Spanish ways of work and life. Both government and religious officials expected the missions eventually to become Spanish towns, with the indigenous population adopting the customs and religious practices of the mother country Spain.

Frederick William Beechey, commander of a British vessel that sailed into San Fran-

tracts of land. Herds of imported livestock had settled in comfortably, reaching to many tens of thousands of cattle, sheep, goats, horses, and mules.

Learning About the Mission Period

Accounts of this period and the changes it brought come mainly from the Spaniards who ran the missions and from other Europeans who sailed along the California coast. The missionaries were required to keep meticulous accounts of everything from natural landscape, to native cultures, to work schedules. While they attempted to be objective, they usually painted a positive picture of mission life.

The journals and reports written by other visitors bring a perspective that complements the friars' reports. During the mission period, only about a dozen English, French, and Russian vessels sailed into California ports, each staying only a few weeks. These visitors lacked the in-depth knowledge of the Spanish padres about mission life. As representatives of governments that were Spain's rivals, most of these visitors followed strict diplomatic protocol but disagreed with Spanish claims to California. In addition, many were not Roman Catholic and disapproved of the religious goals of the missions. As such, their reports often focused on weaknesses in the mission system.

Indians of the time had no written language and few were taught to read or write in Spanish (or in the Latin language used by the church). Only one Indian wrote his account of mission life near the time of the missions. This Indian, Pablo Tac, was born at Mission San Luis Rey de Francia in 1822, traveled to Rome at the end of the mission period when he was ten, and lived in Rome until he died of smallpox before his twentieth birthday. His short account deals mostly with the physical placement of buildings at

Call to Christianize the New World

A few years after Christopher Columbus reached the New World, Pope Alexander VI issued several bulls or statements, in which he underlined the need to bring Christianity to the indigenous population. These began the precedent that gave the government the right and responsibility to establish missions among nonbelievers in Roman Catholicism. In *The Spanish Tradition in America*, Charles Gibson includes the bull Pope Alexander issued on May 4, 1493, in which he addressed the king and queen of Spain:

"Among other works well pleasing to the Divine Majesty and cherished of our heart, this assuredly ranks highest, that in our times especially the Catholic faith and the Christian religion be exalted and be everywhere increased and spread, that the health of souls be cared for and that barbarous nations be overthrown and brought to faith itself. . . . As becomes Catholic kings and princes after earnest consideration of all matters, especially of the rise and spread of the Catholic faith, as was the fashion of your ancestors, kings of renowned memory, you have purposed with the favor of divine clemency to bring under your sway the said mainlands and islands [of the New World] with their residents and inhabitants and to bring them to the Catholic faith."

the mission and what he knew about nonmission native life. Other information written from an Indian point of view is from recollections recorded in the late 1800s or early 1900s, many decades after the end of the mission period.

By piecing together all these various accounts and combining them with archeological findings, historians have managed to construct a picture of life in the California missions for all those who experienced the events.

Founding the Missions

Founding the missions in California required a combination of planning, hard work, and luck. Both church and government officials in Mexico City made extensive preparation for each new mission to be founded in this remote region. When they got to California, mission founders followed the plans as much as possible but often faced unforeseen challenges. In the end, they learned to improvise.

The California missions were built by order of the viceroy. The viceroy was the king's highest permanent official in New Spain, as the colony that stretched from Panama to California was then known. Missionaries and other church officials might try to influence the viceroy, but ordering construction of a new mission was a government decision. Missionaries needed the viceroy's approval for many matters relating to the missions. He had to approve the site chosen for a mission, all building projects, and even the name of each mission. If the mission had to be moved away from a flooding river or closer to good farmlands, or rebuilt after an earthquake, the viceroy needed to give his stamp of approval to this too.

Choosing When and Where

In 1769 the king's special envoy, Don José de Gálvez, convinced the viceroy of the need to build presidios and missions at San Diego and Monterey Bays. Gálvez chose San Diego and Monterey as the first sites because, as far as he knew, they provided the best harbors in California.

Until this time California was practically unknown to the Spanish. Spanish ships had sailed along the coast, but no Spaniards had gone ashore except to take on fresh water. Mapmakers had recently drawn California as an island, and the vast bay at San Francisco was unknown to them because thick fog had hidden its mouth whenever sailors passed by. Not until explorers wandered off course while searching for Monterey did any Spaniards stumble onto San Francisco's bay. They described it as large enough to fit the entire Spanish fleet at once. If foreign ships discovered this huge protected harbor, they might attack Spanish missions in California, or try to create their own settlements on lands that Spain claimed for itself.

The viceroy quickly authorized two additional missions where they could help protect San Francisco Bay: one that would be called San Francisco, near the entry to the bay, and the other at Santa Clara, near the bay's southern tip. As contemporary chronicler, Francisco Palóu explained, the viceroy was pleased with early progress and anxious to continue the settlement of California:

> The good news reached his Excellency [the viceroy] that the expedition by sea and land had arrived at the desired port of Monterey, . . . and had been taken possession of for our king of Spain. . . .

His Excellency the Viceroy, the Marquis de Croix, immediately decided, in accord with the visitor-general, to found . . . [five more missions] between San Diego and the port of . . . San Francisco.

With this object the visitor-general sent for the reverend father guardian of the College [of San Fernando], and informed him of his Excellency's decision in regard to the founding of the missions, and consequently that it would be necessary [to send additional missionaries].[3]

Pinpointing a Perfect Site

Once he decided to start a new mission, the viceroy then commissioned an exploring party to search the general area and recommend a specific site. The exploring party consisted of at least one military officer, several soldiers, and a friar. They took several weeks or even months to scout new territory.

The explorers wanted to learn the general characteristics of the region where they traveled, but they were also looking for specific features in choosing a mission site. The site must be near native villages. After all, the purpose of the mission was to convert the Indians and make them part of the mission's workforce. A perfect site also offered the potential for good farming. Father Juan Crespí described one potential mission site this way:

> It appears to be good arable land, and seems to have marshes or damp soil. The bed of the stream is full of trees, such as

Mission San Francisco, now called Mission Dolores, was built to protect San Francisco Bay. The original church still stands; the basilica (rear) was added in 1876.

Exploring Party

As the military diarist Miguel Costansó explained in his journal, published as *The Discovery of San Francisco Bay: The Portolá Expedition of 1769–1770*, the exploring party could never travel very far or very fast,

"that the marches of [the exploring party] with so great a train and [so many] obstacles, through unknown lands and on unused roads, could not be long. Not to mention other reasons that made it necessary to halt and camp early—the necessity of reconnoitering the country from day to day in order to regulate the marches according to the distance between the watering-places, and consequently to take the proper precautions. Sometimes they resumed their journey in the afternoon immediately after watering the animals, upon the reliable information that on the next stage there was little or no water, or a scarcity of pasture.

Stops were made, as the necessity demanded, at intervals of four days, more or less. . . . It was necessary to accommodate the sick when there were any—and in course of time there were many—whose strength gave way under the continuous fatigue, and the excessive heat and intense cold.

But the pack animals themselves constitute the greatest danger on these journeys, and are the most dreaded enemy —though without them nothing could be accomplished. At night and in a country they do not know, these animals are very easily frightened. The sight of a coyote or a fox is sufficient to stampede them. . . . This expedition, however, suffered no serious detriment on this account, owing to the care and watchfulness that were always observed; and although, on some occasions, the animals were stampeded, no accident or injury whatever followed, because the stampede was of short duration."

willows, poplars, and sycamores, but the river we found dry in many places. . . . We do not know whether this river could be used for irrigation or not, but if it depends on rainfall, as is the case in other parts, good seasonal plantings can be made, for it has plenty of land and good places for cattle with good grass. But in the whole region there is no building stone visible, and it seems that firewood also is scarce in the entire vicinity, as far as can be seen.[4]

At least one person in the exploring party had the job of writing a journal of all they saw. At the end of the exploration, they sent the viceroy a copy of the journal and their recommendations for specific sites. The viceroy usually approved the chosen site.

When the Site Was Imperfect

Despite the best efforts of the exploring parties, sometimes a site turned out to have unforeseen problems. For example, the first site chosen for San Diego was too near the river, which washed away the crops when the winter rains came. In the second year, the San Diego mission was moved to a site too far away from any source of water. Having escaped the flooding of the previous site, now all the crops died in a dry spell. Eventually, the friars found the permanent mission site, where they could tap into the river but not be flooded every rainy season.

Similar problems occurred with other missions. Floods washed out the Santa Clara mission at its first two locations. Like San Diego, the third site for Santa Clara became the permanent one. The La Purísima mission site seemed perfect for many years until 1812, when an earthquake, followed by a mudslide and flood destroyed all the buildings. After that, the mission was completely rebuilt on a site four miles away.

The mission built originally at Monterey was moved within one year across some hills to the banks of the Carmel River, where the lands were better for agriculture. Before moving the mission site, Father Junípero Serra asked for and received permission from the viceroy. As contemporary chronicler Francisco Palóu explained:

[Junípero Serra] had informed his Excellency [the viceroy] that in the port of Monterey there was no running water for irrigating and planting crops for the mission, and that he judged Carmelo [by the Carmel River] to be a better site, for with the waters of the river there the land could be worked, and as it was not more than a league from the royal presidio, he asked his consent to move it. His Excellency replied, giving his consent to the petition to move the mission to the neighborhood of that river, or wherever he thought best.[5]

The Carmel mission as it appears today. The mission, originally established in Monterey, was moved to its present location because the new site offered superior agricultural conditions.

Getting Ready to Go

Once a site was chosen, a founding party traveled to the site to get the mission started. The founding party included friars, at least one government representative, and a few soldiers. From five to fifty Christianized Indians also came along to tend the mules, clear pathways, and do other chores. The Christianized Indians were brought from missions elsewhere in California or, before any of the California missions were established, from Baja California.

The founding party brought with them all the supplies required to live for a year or more. They would need large quantities of food, livestock, seed, tools, and sacred church objects, which they borrowed from existing missions. Before leaving for a new mission site, ships were loaded and mule trains packed with everything from cattle to clothing and candles to chocolate.

Father Francisco Palóu compiled an inventory of the supplies sent with the first ships and overland pack trains to San Diego and Monterey. The ships carried chickens and other small animals, but the livestock went on its own power with the land divisions. Palóu's lists include a total of 200 head of cattle, most of them cows with their calves; 160 saddle and pack mules; 51 good horses, plus a stallion and 6 mares; 58 leather harness sets; and 40 leather water bags. In addition, the land divisions carried large quantities of

> figs, [a caked brown sugar called] panocha, jerked meat, flour, . . . wheat, . . . raisins, [hardtack] biscuit in hampers of green hide, . . . beef tallow, . . . brandy and of wine.

> [A supply ship was] loaded with corn, beans, and chick peas, . . . [ten thousand pounds] of dried meat, some more of fish, [more than one thousand pounds] of figs and raisins, ten jars, two of brandy and the rest of wine, and some bales of coarse clothing, so that they might have something with which to make gifts to the Indians.[6]

A Treacherous First Voyage

The earliest missions were by far the most difficult to found. The founders started their trek from Baja California and elsewhere in Mexico, and traveled for months before arriving in California. So risky was the venture to found California's first missions that four separate divisions of expeditionary forces were sent. Two divisions went by land and two by sea.

The founding parties who traveled by land faced many possible problems. No one knew how long the trip overland from Baja California to San Diego would take. No Spaniard had traveled this path before. Every day, scouts went ahead, looking for the next day's resting place, somewhere with water to drink and pasturage for the animals. All along the way they feared attacks by hostile Indians. They also worried that they might come across some unknown natural barrier, such as a mountain range or river canyon, that would make it impossible to go forward. The Franciscan friar Juan Crespí wrote a journal in which he recorded every day's events. The following passage is a sample entry from this journal:

> April 19. At eight in the morning we set out from the camping place toward the northwest, veering to the west. The journey lasted five hours and a half, in which we must have traveled about five leagues, over a bad [path] of ups and downs and

Diary of the Trip to San Diego

Father Juan Crespí wrote a diary of the first land expedition from Baja California to San Diego. Each day's entry identifies the day in the church calendar, such as Good Friday, Easter, or specific saints' days. It also describes the physical setting: hills, valleys, trees, streams, and rivers. Francisco Palóu included Crespí's diary in his *Historical Memoirs*. Here is a sampling of the entries for the first and last days:

"March 24, 1769, Good Friday. About four in the afternoon, those of us destined for the first division of the expedition set out. . . . We directed our course between some hills. After two hours' traveling we stopped after sunset in a dry [creek bed] which had some grass, and camp was pitched there; we had covered about a league and a half. The country continues . . . sterile, arid, lacking grass and water, and abounding in stones and thorns. . . .

May 14, Sunday, the Feast of Espíritu Santo. Not only did it rain on us all night and thoroughly wet us all, but the morning opened very dark, and as soon as day dawned a heavy shower fell again. . . , which I endured without any other covering than my cloak and hat. . . . The captain was of the opinion that I should not say Mass, because we were all so wet, and also because there was a large crowd of [Indians] standing there, all armed . . . [and because] we were all anxious to reach the desired port. . . . We set out a little before ten o'clock, continuing north. . . . The day's march occupied somewhat more than six hours and a half, all over level land, well covered with grass, during which we probably traveled about six leagues, and we arrived very fortunately and happily at the desired port of San Diego."

gorges. We now found the mountains and hills covered with some small trees similar to the juniper, and small oaks, but the land continued sterile and without grass. Many signs of heathen [Indians] have been seen which indicate that the country is well populated, although the people do not permit themselves to be seen. At five leagues we came to a [creek bed] full of alders and plenty of grass, but without water. . . . We stopped near[by] comforted by the fact that we had brought water for the people in the barrels and leather bags, though the animals were left without any.[7]

The founding parties who traveled by sea faced an even riskier voyage. Either or both ships might sink or be blown hopelessly off course. The ships that transported the missionaries were small and crowded, they rocked mercilessly on high seas, their supplies of food and water were limited and often of poor quality. Seasickness and scurvy plagued many who made the voyage.

All four groups eventually reached San Diego, but the trip north had been treacherous. A trip that takes a day or less in modern times took months in the 1700s. Less than half of the 130 Spaniards survived the voyage. Of the eighty-six Christianized Indians who started the trek, five died en route, and sixty-one reportedly abandoned the trek and returned home. A supply ship, which left a few weeks after the two other transport ships, was disabled in a storm just outside port on its first trip. It took months to repair the ship. When it finally sailed again, it sank at sea with all hands.

Easier with Time

After this first trip, it was never as difficult for a founding party to get to a new mission site. For one thing, the founders learned more about local geography and native culture. In addition, later founding parties could start from an existing mission within California. They could make their preparations, take a mule train to carry the supplies, and travel for just a day or two as opposed to the months-long trips required of the first groups.

By the time the nineteenth mission was founded at Santa Inés, the process had become relatively easy. Military commander Raymundo Carrillo and his soldiers joined four friars and a group of already converted Indians for the thirty-five-mile hike through the coastal mountains from Mission Santa Barbara. They brought with them cattle, sheep, mules, and plenty of food and tools for building and farming.

Starting a Mission from the Ground Up

Creating a mission where nothing had been built before took lots of hard work. The work began almost as soon as the founding party got to the site.

One of the first tasks was to hang the church bell from a nearby tree, or if there were no trees, from a pole pounded into the ground. They also built an altar, where the friars could say mass, and protected the altar with a temporary shelter built of branches. Meanwhile, other members of the founding party set up the camp where people could live until more permanent shelter could be arranged.

Usually within a week of arriving, the friars were ready to say mass and celebrate the founding of the new mission. For the founding date, the friars always chose an important day in the religious calendar. The chosen day might be Easter Sunday, Trinity Sunday, the day of the saint for whom the mission was named, or a day in history when a crusade had been successful in making converts.

Founding Ceremonies

The founding ceremonies reflected the combined effort of the Spanish government and the church. The ceremonies began with mass and blessings for the new undertaking. They concluded with a military flourish.

Early Construction

Pablo Tac was a California Indian who was born and baptized at Mission San Luis Rey in 1822. He traveled to Italy when he was ten and died there of smallpox before he was twenty. In his account of mission life, called *Indian Life and Customs at Mission San Luis Rey: A Record of California Mission Life,* Tac described what he had heard from his parents and the friars about early construction at Mission San Luis Rey.

"[The Indians] could understand [the friar] somewhat when he, as their father, ordered them to carry stone from the sea (which is not far) for the foundations, to make bricks, roof tiles, to cut beams, reeds and what was necessary . . . and within a few years they finished working."

Father Junípero Serra figured prominently in the establishment of the California missions.

The friars wore their most elegant vestments and made prominent display of polished silver chalices and candlesticks. Military officers donned their best uniforms. Soldiers fired muskets and cannons repeatedly. Friars or their servants rang the church bells as loudly as possible.

Father Junípero Serra described the founding of the second mission, San Carlos Borromeo de Carmelo, at Monterey this way:

> The day arrived. A chapel and altar were constructed. . . .
>
> When all were kneeling before the altar I intoned the "Veni Creator Spiritus." . . . We all assisted in raising [a large cross] and I blessed it. . . . Then we planted it in the ground. . . . With holy water I blessed those fields. The ceremony being

accompanied by shouts of "Long live the faith!" and "Long live the King!" Added to this was the clangor of the bells, the volleys of the muskets, and the cannonading from the [ship].

> After this I began the High Mass to which I added the sermon on the Gospel of the day. All the while there was cannonading. . . .
>
> At the end, standing, I intoned the "Te Deum Laudamus." . . . The officers conducted the ceremony of taking possession of that land in the name of His Catholic Majesty, setting up again and waving the royal standard, pulling up grass, removing stones, and conducting the ceremonies prescribed by law, accompanied by the shouts of "Viva!", bells, and musket shots.[8]

The friars hoped that the color and sounds of the ceremony would attract the attention of Indians to the mission. The friars knew from experience that this was a good way to start their recruitment efforts. It was not uncommon, however, that Indians who had ventured near to investigate the activity were scared into hiding for days or weeks after all the noise and clamor.

Preparing for the Future

After the church bells stopped ringing and the smoke from the muskets drifted away, everybody got out of their fancy clothes and rolled up their sleeves. They had a lot of work to do to get a new mission started.

The California missions were expected to be self-sufficient. Within five years of its founding, each mission was supposed to produce enough to feed, clothe, and house its own population. With this goal in mind, crops were planted and livestock pastured almost as soon as the temporary altar was erected.

In the years until sufficient crops could be harvested reliably, people at a new mission relied on help from other missions. For example, in a letter to the missionaries of California written in March 1785, Juan Sancho, guardian of the College of San Fernando, warned:

> For the founding of the Mission of Santa Barbara, it is necessary that all the Missions concur in supplying domestic animals of every kind, and also seed grain; for such is the royal disposition which

must be observed without the least objection on the part of any missionary.[9]

The first missions did not have this option, however. Instead, they depended on annual shipments from Baja California and mainland Mexico to provide food, tools, and other supplies. Shipments from Mexico continued to supply the California missions until about 1810 (when the outbreak of Mexico's war for independence disrupted the traffic). By then, the missions had become less and less reliant on outside support. They could grow or make most of what they needed thanks to the mild climate, fertile soil, and plenty of people to farm the land and tend the livestock.

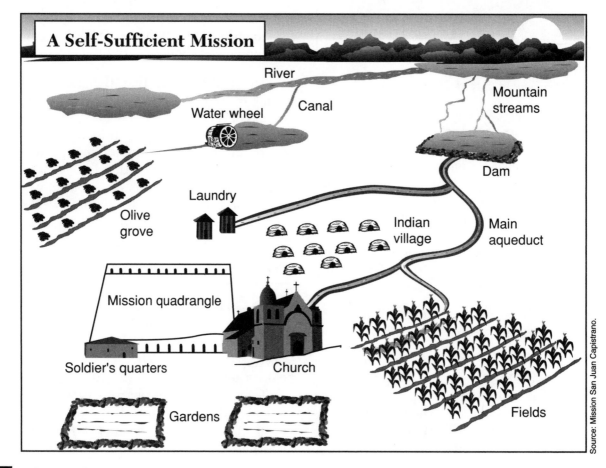

A Self-Sufficient Mission

River
Water wheel
Canal
Mountain streams
Dam
Olive grove
Laundry
Indian village
Main aqueduct
Mission quadrangle
Soldier's quarters
Church
Gardens
Fields

Source: Mission San Juan Capistrano.

This re-creation of an early Indian home is on display at Mission San Juan Capistrano.

However, there was always a demand for metal tools, which were difficult to produce locally. The following letter, which Santa Barbara missionary Antonio Ripoll wrote to the governor of California on May 9, 1817, provides an example of what they needed.

"Just now we are in need of various articles, such as carpenter's tools, a forge, files, chisels, large saw, etc. I shall appreciate it very much if you could send these things in exchange for the goods forwarded to you. . . . If not, we shall again have to practice patience." [10]

Building Shelter for Body and Soul

The first buildings at a new mission included shelter for the friars and the military guards, and a small chapel. Then came workrooms and storerooms, followed by housing for the Indians. These first structures were built of

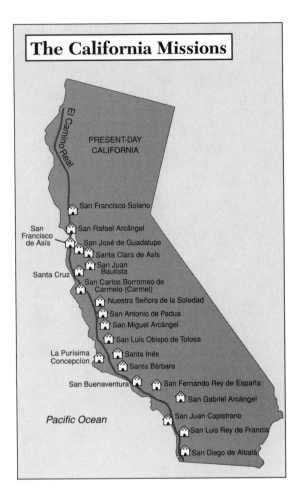

The California Missions

El Camino Real

PRESENT-DAY
CALIFORNIA

San Francisco Solano

San Rafael Arcángel

San
Francisco
de Asís

San José de Guadalupe

Santa Clara de Asís

San Juan
Bautista

Santa Cruz

San Carlos Borromeo de
Carmelo (Carmel)

Nuestra Señora de la Soledad

San Antonio de Padua

San Miguel Arcángel

San Luis Obispo de Tolosa

La Purísima
Concepción

Santa Inés

Santa Bárbara

San Buenaventura

San Fernando Rey de España

San Gabriel Arcángel

San Juan Capistrano

San Luis Rey de Francia

San Diego de Alcalá

Pacific Ocean

structures of adobe and tile were begun almost immediately at Mission Solano, and mission gardens were bearing fruit within the first two years.

Building for Success

One of the most important reasons for ongoing building projects was the very success of a mission. Within a few years of its founding, a mission was home to hundreds of people. These people needed houses to live in, a church to pray in, storerooms, workshops, kitchens, and more.

Nearly all the missions followed the same basic design, called a quadrangle. The quadrangle was a design that had been used in Europe for centuries. The quadrangle was roughly shaped like a hollow square. Rows of buildings on four sides enclosed an open-air patio or courtyard. The quadrangle provided security from outside intruders while creating a centralized location in which the friars could control mission activities. Living quarters for the friars and the children, and storerooms, warehouses, and workrooms were all part of the quadrangle. The church was also located there. It was the most refined edifice at a mission. Most of the churches had beamed roofs, high ceilings, and painted walls.

Mission Accomplished

In just over sixty years from the time the king of Spain's special envoy Don José de Gálvez urged that two missions be built in California, a total of twenty-one missions had been founded. This represented a huge accomplishment, achieved despite challenges that included locating good sites, sending supplies, constructing buildings, and attracting both missionaries and local people.

tree trunks and branches. They were covered with mud and roofed with more branches or the long tule grasses found in the wetlands.

Early buildings rarely lasted longer than a few years. Mud roofs washed out in the rain, and tules and timber often burned or rotted. Soon they learned to use clay that was found nearby to make sun-dried bricks, called adobes. Eventually most mission buildings were made of these adobes, and were covered with clay tile roofs.

As in other matters, even construction was easier for the later missions. For example, building was fast and efficient at Mission Solano, the last mission founded. Permanent

The Making of a Missionary

Becoming a missionary in California required both courage and a strong spiritual grounding. Visiting California in 1786, the French nobleman and scientist Count Jean-François de Galoup de La Pérouse described the friars of the California missions as "true" missionaries, "who have abandoned the idle life of a cloister [monastery] to give themselves up to fatigues, cares, and anxieties of every kind."[11]

Choosing a Religious Life

The friars who came to California were born and reared in Spain, where religion was an important and integral part of everyday life. Most Spaniards were Catholic and attended mass regularly. They believed that God had chosen their king and granted him a divine right to rule. The Catholic Church provided basic social services, including schools, hospitals, and charity for the poor.

Because of the importance and prestige of the Catholic religion, many boys felt the calling to leave home and join the church. Junípero Serra, who later became a powerful force in the California missions, was so impressed by his education in church and the men he met there that he decided early on to become a missionary. His friend and biographer, Francisco Palóu, described Serra's early years this way:

His pious parents instructed him from his infancy in the rudiments of the faith and in the holy fear of God, [encouraging] him, from the time he was able to walk, to attend frequently the church and convent . . . in the village. The boy's father was well liked by the friars and whenever he took his son . . . with him to the Convent, the boy won the affection of all. Here is where he learned Latin, in which he soon became very proficient, and at the same time he became skilled in plain chanting. . . . From this holy exercise and from the pious conversations which he heard from the good Fathers, there was born in his heart a very earnest desire, even at an early age, to [join the Church].[12]

Most young men who joined the church became parish priests and worked in the churches of Spain. It was their job to serve the Catholic population of their parish by celebrating mass, hearing confessions, and performing baptisms, marriages, and other duties at church and in the community.

Some of those who did not become parish priests joined a religious order, such as the Franciscans, instead. The founders of many religious orders believed that the best way to venerate God was to live inside monasteries, completely isolated from the outside world. They spent their days in quiet, sometimes silent contemplation, gardening, reading, and praying.

Franciscans

Saint Francis of Assisi, who founded the Franciscan order in the early 1200s, believed that

Junípero Serra

Father Junípero Serra's religious zeal and single-minded energy were largely responsible for starting the chain of missions in California. He was born on November 24, 1713, in the town of Petra on the island of Mallorca, Spain. His first application to become a Franciscan was rejected because, being small and sickly, he seemed too young to become a novice. He applied again and convinced a former teacher to argue his case until eventually he was successful.

As his friend and biographer, Francisco Palóu explains in the *Life and Apostolic Labors of the Venerable Father Junípero Serra,* Serra surprised his community when he decided to give up the success he had achieved as a preacher and a teacher of philosophy to become a missionary at the age of thirty-six:

"At this time in which the Reverend Father Lector Fr. Junípero was enjoying the highest esteem and applause, both from friars and others, and when it might be expected that the corresponding honors would come to him as a matter of merit, the voice of God came to him, calling him to be a teacher of the pagans, touching his heart and leading him to leave his native land, his parents, and his holy Province, in order to employ his talents in the conversion of the pagans who, for lack of someone to show them the way to heaven, were perishing. He was not un-mindful of this secret voice of the Lord which lighted in his heart the fire of love for his fellow men and gave birth in him to the most vivid desire to shed his blood, if necessary, in order to secure the salvation of the miserable gentiles, and reviving in his heart those desires which he had felt when a novice, which had been deadened somewhat by the distraction of his studies."

Father Junípero Serra enjoyed the high regard of his community in Spain, but, at age thirty-six, he sensed the voice of God calling him to serve as a missionary.

isolated contemplation was not sufficient for a religious order. Saint Francis taught that a true religious life should include not only quiet contemplation and prayer, but also work in the world outside the monastery walls.

The people who became missionaries in California were members of the Franciscan order, one of the largest and most active religious orders in Spain at the time. Many Franciscans stayed in Spain and worked at a variety of jobs there, including serving as parish priests. Some pursued an academic life, teaching, researching, and writing at one of Spain's Catholic universities.

A few Franciscans became missionaries, volunteering to live and work among non-Catholics in California, or elsewhere in the Americas, or in Asia or Africa. The work of a missionary was to convert people to Catholicism. This, they believed, would save souls and allow converts into Heaven.

Disciplined Life of a Novice

The young men who wished to work as missionaries in California first needed to be trained in the basics of the order, then accepted as a Franciscan, and then pursue several more years of training.

As a first step, a teenage boy applied to become a novice at any time after his sixteenth birthday. Superiors in the order interviewed the young man to determine if they thought he was serious about wanting to join. If his application was accepted, he became a novice for at least one year.

This year, called the novitiate, was the time when he learned to live the regimented life of a Franciscan and to follow the Rule that Saint Francis set forth for his followers. Specifically, according to the Rule, a Franciscan vowed to obey his superiors, to remain chaste, and to live a life of material poverty. Except under exceptional circumstances, Franciscans were forbidden to wear shoes, ride on horseback or in carriages, or own any personal items. As one Franciscan official explained in 1835, they took the vow of poverty "in order to disentangle ourselves from all worldly cares and occupy our minds with the exercise of charity and holy prayer."[13]

Final Vows

At the end of the yearlong novitiate, a novice was prepared to make a final decision about joining the order permanently. A few novices left when they found the rigors of religious life too difficult, but most continued through the full year and then took their final vows and became friars. Becoming a friar in the Franciscan order was a lifetime commitment, not a decision to be taken lightly.

This sculpture depicts a novice missionary. Novices took the vow of poverty and learned to live the very restricted life of a Franciscan.

After taking final vows a Franciscan continued his daily cycle of spiritual activities and religious studies. He also took on new responsibilities. Friars worked at the monastery, or in a school or university. They also worked to maintain the monastery by gardening there, cooking, or keeping accounts.

After a few years in the order, most friars also became ordained priests. As priests, they could celebrate mass, deliver sermons, and hear confessions. They could also perform baptisms, marriages, and last rites. Priests needed to be able to act with maturity and to possess a solid religious training. Thus, while a young man could become a Franciscan when he was still a teenager, he could not be ordained into the priesthood until he was at least twenty-four years old.

Volunteering for Missionary Work

Missionary work was voluntary for Franciscans. In fact, most Franciscans preferred to stay in Spain, where they led meaningful religious lives without leaving everything that was familiar to them.

Poor Clares

No women were allowed into the Franciscan order that supplied missionaries to California. However, one of the three Franciscan orders is an order for women: the Second Order of Saint Francis, Poor Ladies, Sisters of Saint Clare—or just, Poor Clares. They are named Poor because of their strict vow of poverty, and Clares for their founder, Saint Clare of Assisi.

Saint Clare was the first woman to found an order. Born in 1194, Clare was an Italian of noble birth who decided to give up her worldly goods and start a convent after she heard the preaching of Saint Francis, the founder of the Franciscans. Clare's father had hoped to make a good marriage for her and was disappointed at first when she chose a strictly religious life. She was able to convince her father of the importance of her calling, and soon her mother, a sister, an aunt, and a niece joined Clare in the convent.

Unlike the Franciscan friars who came to California, the Poor Clares believe in a life of cloistered contemplation, living in isolation from the world. No Poor Clares came to the New World during the mission period.

Saint Clare kneels with Saint Francis of Assisi at her side. Saint Clare was born into a noble family but renounced all trappings of privilege and started a convent.

Missionaries conduct a special processional at a California mission. The most successful friars were able to adapt to the hardships that everyone in California faced.

Most friars who volunteered for missionary work were in their late twenties. By the time he was in his mid-thirties, a friar was considered too old to begin a missionary career.

Some friars had always wanted to become missionaries. Others decided to volunteer after listening to the Franciscan emissaries who returned from Mexico to recruit new missionaries from among the friars in Spain. New missionaries were needed to fill vacancies left when an old missionary retired, died, or was transferred. Sometimes they were needed to fill posts created as the mission system expanded into new territories, as was the case for California in the late 1700s. When more

missionaries were needed, Franciscan representatives returned to Spain to recruit them. They visited Franciscan colleges and convents, describing the glories, challenges, and opportunities of missionary work.

The recruiters were looking for friars who wanted to go to New Spain and those who could be successful there. The friars who were most successful were the ones who did not mind the rough living conditions and isolation. As Junípero Serra later explained, good missionaries were "subjects who do not turn their backs on hardships, and who do not become restless and anxious to return . . . almost as soon as they arrive here. Those who come here dedicated to so holy a work must undergo hardships, as everyone knows. . . . In these distant parts, one must expect to undergo some hardships, but these will be even more burdensome to those who are seeking every convenience and comfort."[14]

Hazardous Duty

The recruiters' task was not always easy because missionary work was difficult and sometimes dangerous. The people who volunteered knew that they might lose their lives working among Indians who hated the Franciscans for intruding into Indian territory. The friars who went to California had heard the stories about Indians attacking and killing Franciscans at missions in Texas and elsewhere. A few volunteers actually looked forward to possible martyrdom while doing the Lord's work because this meant that they would go directly to Heaven. Most preferred to look forward to a long life and a nonviolent death.

Even among those who volunteered for missionary work, California was not a top choice. Because California was the newest chain of Franciscan missions, conditions there were more difficult than in already established mission communities. Few local inhabitants spoke Spanish or understood Spanish customs. And, especially in the beginning, there were no houses to live in, churches to pray in, or familiar foods to eat.

The local inhabitants and primitive living conditions were not the only worry for missionaries. They were also concerned about their spiritual lives. Many feared that even though their faith was deep, they might be corrupted by worldly temptations. They feared that living so far from the watchful eye of their community, they might be tempted to break their vows of obedience, chastity, and poverty. They also feared that they might die without receiving last rites.

Red Tape

It was never a young man's independent decision to become a missionary. He needed to request permission from his superiors in the order, from the recruiter, and from the Spanish government. Usually, the recruiter was the easiest to convince, as it was always difficult to find enough volunteers. However, a friar's immediate superiors could present more of a challenge. When a friar left, someone else was needed to take over the job he had been doing at his home friary in Spain. It usually took months, and sometimes several years, before a friar could get approval to leave.

Francisco Palóu, in his biography of Junípero Serra, outlines how he and Serra applied for missionary work. Among other obstacles, he mentions that while Palóu and Serra were from the island of Mallorca, the recruiters preferred missionaries from the Spanish mainland. Also, their superior in Mallorca apparently destroyed the recruiters' original acceptance letter, as he did not want to lose two of his valuable friars.

> [Serra] wrote to the Reverend Commissioners General of the Order and of the Indies, asking them to take part in the conversion of the pagans. The Commissioners replied to him, saying that his appointment was impossible because [the recruiters] had completed their work . . . and were on the eve of embarking. However, he said he would bear our request in mind for the very first occasion, adding that it might be an obstacle in our way that we did not belong to the peninsula of Spain. . . .

He wrote again to the Commissioners begging them that if the fact that he was an islander presented a real difficulty, that he be permitted to enter into some one of the Colleges of the peninsula of Spain in order to overcome this obstacle. . . .

Our Rev. Father Commissioner General of the Indies, Fr. Matias Velasco, did not forget our request. . . . He sent it to the [recruiters]. The letter arrived very opportunely, for out of the thirty-three friars who had enlisted for the Missions of [the College of San Fernando], five had repented on account of their fear of the sea which they had never seen. For this reason room was made for us. . . . Immediately the next day we set about carrying out our plans for the voyage. [15]

Setting Out for the New World

The journey to New Spain brought numerous physical and psychological challenges. Leaving a world that was familiar to them was only the first of the many challenges. The voyage across the Atlantic to Mexico was the next.

Once or twice a year, recruits traveled from all over Spain to the southern port of Cádiz. Here, they boarded the ships that took them away from Spain. The fear of transatlantic travel made several would-be missionaries change their minds after they had

Young friars faced a long journey by ship to New Spain, and some, overcome by fear of traveling such a distance, chose not to embark.

arrived at Cádiz. For most young friars, this was the first time they saw the sea or would have traveled by ship.

The transatlantic crossing could take two months or more. This is how Francisco Palóu described the voyage that he took with Junípero Serra from Spain to the port of Veracruz in Mexico:

> On the 28th of August of the year 1749 the first group of enlisted friars embarked. . . . In the long voyage of ninety-nine days which we spent in reaching Vera Cruz there were not lacking vexations and alarms, because in the small space of the vessel there had to be accommodated not only our company but also that of the Reverend Dominican Fathers, besides the other passengers, and also because, fifteen days before reaching Puerto Rico, there was a scarcity of water and the ration had to be diminished (the amount given for the twenty-four hours was but little more than a quart).[16]

From Veracruz, the friars bound for missionary work hiked the 250 miles (and five thousand feet in elevation) to the Apostolic College of San Fernando in Mexico City.

College of San Fernando

The new arrivals were well versed in religious matters but ignorant about the practicalities of mission work. What they did not know yet was how to live on the frontier, how to communicate with non-Spanish speakers, and how to recruit and convert native Californians to Christianity. Friars needed to be charismatic leaders, able to recruit and convert natives. They also needed as many practical frontier survival skills as possible.

It was at the Apostolic College of San Fernando in Mexico City where they learned many of these skills. San Fernando was one of four Franciscan missionary colleges in Mexico. Each college ran the missions in one or more specific regions (such as Texas or Baja California). California was one of the regions directed by the College of San Fernando.

Each new missionary needed to learn at least the rudiments of agriculture, architec-

A Spanish Visitor's Thoughts on the College of San Fernando

José Cardero, scribe on the Spanish vessels that visited Monterey in 1792, believed that the College of San Fernando did not prepare the friars adequately. His description appears in Donald C. Cutter's *California in 1792: A Spanish Naval Visit*.

"[At the] College of San Fernando they should equip the [friars] with the proper instruction for making the Californians not only Christians but also useful to society and the state, to provide them with an enjoyable life. . . . The [friars] sent to California should be taught methodically under good teachers the languages of those barbarian nations with whom they are to deal. . . . And since they are to be the directors of physical efforts, they should have acquired a knowledge of agriculture, stock raising, the tools most useful for the cultivation of the fields, the easiest way to spin, weave, and so on."

An engraving depicts Mexico City in the early eighteenth century. The city was home to the Apostolic College of San Fernando, one of four Franciscan missionary colleges in Mexico.

ture, animal husbandry, hydro-engineering, tile making, stone masonry, carpentry, food preparation, and weaving. Ideally they would have a year or more at the college to learn these skills before being assigned to a mission. However, depending on the immediate needs in the field, some only stayed at the college a few months. In any case, no amount of book learning could fully prepare a friar for the rigors of missionary work.

Even after the missionaries arrived in California, they continued to improve their skills. Both from reading and from practical hands-on experience, they learned about matters of daily importance: everything from Indian languages, to health care, to crop rotation, to building in a land of earthquakes. Several of the missions had large libraries with a thousand or more volumes, including practical books on farming, livestock hus-

bandry, engineering, and interior decoration for churches.

In addition to its educational role, San Fernando served as a home away from home for many of the young missionaries. Here they could rest after the long voyage from Spain, or recuperate from illness. To ease the transition, a young missionary generally was paired with someone who was more experienced and could act as a mentor. Mentors offered both spiritual and practical guidance.

Daily Life at the College

The College of San Fernando was both home and school to as many as one hundred friars at any one time. Daily life at the college was tightly structured, with no time for idle conversation.

The college day started at midnight, when all of the friars filed into the chapel to chant, to meditate, and to recite the set of prayers written for these early hours, called matins. Then they returned to bed from 2 to 5 A.M., when they arose again for another round of prayers and chanting. Before they left the chapel, they participated in a private mass for college residents, and a public mass for local parishioners. After a light breakfast, which consisted of a cup of chocolate and a piece of bread, the day's classes began. The friars studied theology and religious history, as well as practical skills including Indian languages, recruitment techniques, and how to run a mission. At noontime they visited the chapel for brief prayers and ate their most substantial meal of the day, usually a meat or vegetable stew. After a nap (siesta), they returned to their studies and then back to chapel for another round of prayer and meditation. At about 7 P.M. they ate a light supper and were in bed by 8 P.M. for a few hours of sleep before the routine began again at midnight.

While at the college, friars were supposed to concentrate on their studies and not be distracted by people and events in the outside world. The college also reinforced the discipline the friars had learned during the novitiate. Friars could not leave the college unless they received permission from the guardian, who was the highest-ranking Franciscan at the college. Most friars never ventured outside the college until it was time to leave for missionary work.

Staying On

Missionaries signed up to remain in California for a ten-year assignment. The average stay was sixteen years, but a few left within their first year and some stayed forty years or more and

An older friar comforts a young Indian boy. Missionaries were expected to remain in California for ten years, although some stayed much longer.

eventually died in California of old age. When French visitor Auguste Duhaut-Cilly visited the Santa Barbara mission in 1827, he found

> An old, feeble Padre was sitting there, a man whom age and infirmity had rendered so indifferent to all that happened around him, that he hardly noticed that we were strangers when we greeted him and inquired about his health. I saw that you had to put your hand heavily upon him to rouse him.[17]

Those who did not complete their ten-year commitment usually left because of ill health. Most of their ailments can be traced to the physical and emotional hardships of living on the frontier. Common complaints included eye troubles, violent headaches, stomach disorders, arthritis, and depression. Two friars were sent back to Mexico for scandalous conduct, which reportedly included staying up late every night drinking, dancing, and singing, while they completely ignored their work responsibilities during the day.

Companionship and Moral Support

Every Franciscan mission had two missionaries to provide each other with companionship and spiritual support on the frontier. As the Spanish official Don José de Gálvez wrote in 1768, "the Franciscan missionaries want to live two to a mission because their order lives in communities and so they can help each other when sick and in spiritual administration."[18]

When possible, a mission's two friars were selected from the same region in Spain. While all the friars were Franciscans, they came from different parts of Spain, where they had spoken different dialects and eaten different foods as children. This way, it would be easier for them to work and relax together.

Father Junípero Serra, who apparently did not mind the other hardships of life on the frontier, insisted on the importance of companionship. His greatest fear was not that he would die or be killed there but that he would die without receiving last rites. He is quoted as saying,

> If someday I shall have to face any personal hardship, it will be this one, namely the great hardship for a sinner like me to remain in such a solitude realizing that the nearest priest will be more than eighty leagues away and between us there will be land inhabited only by pagans with the roads pretty rough.[19]

A Few Dedicated Men

The dedicated men who became friars in the California missions were trained to live and work on the frontier, far from home. Despite the importance of the mission system, only about

Crespí's Plea for Companionship

Ever polite, Father Crespí asked his superiors to consider sending his former colleague, Father Cruzado, to serve as the second friar at the Carmel mission. His request appears in Herbert Eugene Bolton, *Fray Juan Crespí, Missionary Explorer on the Pacific Coast 1769–1774*.

"I begged you to grant me the consolation, when the mission shall have arrived from Spain, and ministers shall have come to bear us company, of favoring me by permitting my companion, Father Cruzado, . . . to come to join me. He desires it very much, as he told me before we separated, but he did not come then because not more than one could come from each mission, as was done. We have been companions for a long time, and there is much he could do here."

forty friars were ever serving in California at one time. Fewer than 130 men served as friars in California during the entire mission period.

This is the way Maynard Geiger, a Franciscan scholar specializing in the history of California missions, describes the men who came to California as missionaries:

By far the greater number persevered with the fidelity to their vows of priesthood and Franciscan life. At the top we find the leaders, men of talent, ability, and eminent virtue, who accomplished great things against overwhelming odds, six of whom sacrificed their lives, while most were in dangerously exposed conditions. The preponderance might be classed as men of ordinary ability, zeal, learning, and virtue. They were good and faithful workers. [20]

The Franciscan friars came to California to convert native Californians to the Roman Catholic faith. The friars believed that the soul of every person who was not Catholic was condemned to eternal damnation in the afterlife. Therefore, the friars believed they were literally saving souls.

First Contact

The Indians, on the other hand, had no knowledge of Roman Catholicism and almost no experience with fair-skinned Europeans. In some native communities, elders told stories of the early Spanish and English explorers. These were stories of bearded, fair-skinned men arriving by sea in huge vessels. The stories passed down from generation to generation and took on the quality of myths. Many years before, their ancestors may have encountered Spanish explorers led by Juan Rodríguez Cabrillo who landed on the Pacific Coast in 1542, or Sebastián Viscaíno in 1603. Some may have met the English explorer Sir Francis Drake and his men in 1579. Since the mid-1700s, some may have seen the few Russian ships that had sailed the California coastal waters hunting for otters and searching for food.

To the Indians, the Spaniards' ships seemed like floating houses in comparison to their own reed or wooden-plank canoes. Muskets, cannons, and other firearms were completely new to them. Men on horseback seemed the size of bears.

Diarist Miguel Costansó, who traveled with the original exploring party from San Diego to Monterey, found that Indians in different areas responded quite differently to the Spaniards. For example, this is how he described one group near present-day Santa Barbara:

The ship of Englishman Sir Francis Drake. California Indians may have encountered Drake and his crew in 1579.

After a short time, the natives of the three towns came with roasted and fresh fish, seeds, acorns, . . . and various other foods, earnestly inviting us to eat, and showing in their faces the pleasure that our presence gave them. We treated them all kindly, and gave them glass beads, ribbons, and other trifles, in exchange for which we received various curios, such as baskets, furs, and [feathers].[21]

However, in another diary entry, Costansó described how a group of some five hundred Indians near Monterey reacted quite differently when they first saw the Spaniards: "These Indians had no notice of our coming to their lands, as our men could see from the consternation and fright that our presence caused: amazed and confused, without knowing what they did, some ran for their weapons, others shouted and yelled, and the women burst into tears."[22]

California Before the Missions

Life in California had changed little for many generations. Native Californians belonged to small nation-states that anthropologists call tribelets. Tribelets varied in size, from about fifty members to five hundred or more. Frequently, neighboring tribelets were unable to communicate with each other. California natives spoke dozens of mutually unintelligible languages and dialects, some as different from each other as Chinese and English.

Individual members of the tribelets did not own land. Like air, land and water were to be shared by all. No one person could buy, sell, or own the lands or waterways. However, each tribelet claimed the right to live in a specific territory. Neighboring tribelets had little contact with each other, although some-

times a young man from one tribelet married a young woman from another.

Conflicts could arise when one tribelet went into another's territory to hunt, fish, or gather food. Community elders were usually able to settle the disputes but sometimes one tribelet attacked another. Warfare was not formal or organized but skirmishes between rival tribelets were not uncommon.

Members of a tribelet lived together in village settlements. Their houses were made of materials available locally including wood, reeds, thatch, and mud, with beds of woven mats or animal skins. Most housed a single family but some were big enough to be shared. Houses were designed to be abandoned when the Indians moved to new territory in search of fresh sources of food.

Over many generations, native Californians had learned to make use of the abundant wildlife and natural objects that surrounded them. They made tools from stone, shell, bone, or wood. They ate well from foods that they could gather (acorns, grass seeds, and pine nuts were staples), fish, or hunt. They used animal pelts, reeds, and grasses for blankets, bedding, and clothing. They wove baskets so tightly, they could be used for storing water and cooking. (In some areas they used pitch from a tree or tar to make the baskets watertight.) In the south, Indians built oceangoing canoes from wooden planks, lashed together with string made from animal skins and sealed with tar. In other regions, some Indians lashed bundles of reeds to make canoes that stayed afloat and traveled swiftly on rivers, in the ocean, and on San Francisco Bay.

Native Californians had no domesticated plants or animals but they did manipulate their natural environment in one significant way. Once a year, or once every few years, they burned their lands. Such controlled burns kept the brush low and promoted the

Before the arrival of the missionaries, California's Indians belonged to tribelets and lived in settlements such as this one.

growth of new saplings by eliminating grasses and small shrubs that competed for sunlight and nutrients. This way, California natives also greatly reduced the risk of a devastating out-of-control forest fire that might be sparked by lightning.

The native Californians were generally healthy. Illness and pain were prevented or cured with herbs, sweat baths, and by ritual treatment. The shamans were among the most respected people of each tribelet. They served the combined roles of priest and doctor. Shamans understood the native world of spiritual beliefs as well as the natural world of plants, animals, and herbs that could be used in health care.

Culture Clash and Misunderstanding

At first, the Indians and the friars had little in common. They spoke different languages, ate different foods, followed different customs.

Native Californians were used to bathing daily but the Spaniards bathed infrequently, fearing that too many baths would make them sick. Both missionaries and the Spanish soldiers who accompanied them wore clothes that covered their arms, legs, and bodies from the neck down. They generally wore the same clothes day after day. Indian dress varied between regions and with different seasons but frequently the men and boys went about nearly naked, and women and girls wore just a skirt.

The Indians' lack of knowledge about farming and the absence of settled occupations such as carpentry or brickmaking were especially jarring to Spanish eyes. The Spaniards simply did not understand how any people could exist without blacksmiths, bankers, shopkeepers, and the like. They saw the Indians as lazy and even stupid, as shown in the following excerpt from José Cardero's 1792 diary:

The basis of the character of the Californians is composed of stupidity and

Pablo Tac, a neophyte at the San Luis Rey Mission until he turned ten, learned from his parents and the mission friars about mission life. In *Indian Life and Customs*, Tac recorded what he had heard about the time when the Spanish first arrived in the region of San Luis Rey.

"When the missionary arrived in our country with a small troop, our captain [chief] and also the others were astonished, seeing them from afar, but they did not run away or seize arms to kill them, but having sat down, they watched them. But when [the Spanish] drew near, then the captain got up . . . and met them. They halted, and the missionary then began to speak, the captain saying perhaps in his language 'hichsom iva haluon, pullucha-jam cham quinai.' 'What is it that you seek here? Get out of our country!' But [the friars] did not understand him, and they answered him in Spanish, and the captain began with signs, and the [friar] gave [the captain] girls and in this manner made him his friend."

insensibility; lack of knowledge and reflection; inconsistency and fickleness; of a will and of appetites without control, without knowledge and even without objective; laziness and terror of all work; perpetual adhesion to all types of pleasure and to childish and brutal entertainment; fearfulness and weakness of spirit; and finally, a miserable lack of everything that makes men, that is rational, political, and useful to themselves and to society.[23]

Communication between the Spaniards and the native Californians was severely hampered because they shared no common language. When the missionaries ventured out into new territories, they usually brought along Indians who had already converted to Christianity to serve as interpreters. However, in California this technique was of little use. There were so many different languages, Indians from one mission were unlikely to be able to speak to those at another mission. In fact, it was not uncommon for many dialects or languages to be spoken in the area around any one mission.

Vicente Santa María, a young Franciscan on an early expedition in the San Francisco Bay area, described his attempts to communicate with natives in this way:

I began to speak to them for a short time, though I knew they could not understand me unless God should work a miracle. All the time that I was speaking, these Indians, silent and attentive, were as if actually comprehending, showing by their faces much satisfaction and joy. When I had finished speaking, I said to those who had come with me that we should sing the "Alabado." [Soon,] there was a great hubbub among the Indians, for some of them had come with two kinds of hot *atole* and some *pinoles*, and they gave all their attention to urging our participation in the feast. So our chorus stopped singing, and we gave the Indians the pleasure they wished, which was that we should eat. After the sailors had finished with the supper that our hosts had brought, I called to the Indian who seemed to me the head man and, taking his hand, began to move it in the sign of the cross, and he, without resisting, began repeating my words with so great clearness that I stood amazed and so did those who were with me.[24]

Strategies for Recruiting

The missionaries were not discouraged by differences in language and culture. They had absolute confidence in the righteousness of their cause. Their first priority on arriving at the site of a potential new mission was to attract the attention of the native people. To do this, they walked among the Indians near

A compelling statue of Father Junípero Serra, the charismatic leader whose zeal inspired other friars in the missionary movement.

the site, knowing that their mere presence would stir interest.

Father Junípero Serra's energy and self-confidence set a standard other missionaries tried to follow. As leader of the early mission movement, he was among the most charismatic missionaries and notoriously confident in his duty to convert the natives to Catholicism. Even those who knew him were surprised by the exuberance he showed in attracting potential converts. On arriving at the site of a new mission, Father Serra would start clanging the church bell that his companions hung from a nearby tree. Even if no Indians came immediately, he would proceed in celebrating services, and rouse the soldiers, servants, and others in his party to sing with him.

Fishing for Souls

The friars understood that they could not teach the Indians about Christianity without repeated and lengthy exposure. Thus once the missionaries got the Indians' attention, they worked to keep it. The friars enticed the Indians to spend more time at the mission, knowing that this would lead to greater interest in adopting Catholicism.

The enticements varied. At first the missionaries just tried to appear friendly and make the mission a pleasant place. With gifts, smiles, and friendly gestures, the missionaries wanted to show that they were not dangerous. Indians who came to take a peek were given small gifts. Most missionaries started by giving glass beads, food, or cloth to anyone who came to the mission site. The friars gave larger gifts to those who returned to the mission repeatedly or brought their friends. Indians who helped with work were given even more.

Forceful Persuasion

Frederick William Beechey, commander of a British ship that sailed into San Francisco Bay in 1826, described what he understood of the recruiting and conversion process. Beechey's report is included in Joshua Paddison's *A World Transformed: Firsthand Accounts of California Before the Gold Rush*.

"The Indians are brought to the mission. They are placed under the [instruction] of some of the most enlightened of their countrymen, who teach them to repeat in Spanish the Lord's Prayer and certain passages in the [Roman Catholic] litany, and also, to cross themselves properly on entering the church. In a few days, a willing Indian becomes proficient in these mysteries and suffers himself to be baptized and duly initiated into the church. If, however, as it not infrequently happens, any of the captured Indians show a repugnance to conversion, it is the practice to imprison them for a few days and then to allow them to breathe a little fresh air in a walk 'round the mission, to observe the happy mode of life of their converted countrymen; after which they are again shut up, and thus continue to be incarcerated until they declare their readiness to renounce the religion of their forefathers."

The guardian of the College of San Fernando explained the strategy of offering gifts as a means of enticement, likening it to a fishing expedition: "[Gifts of beads, trinkets, food, and clothing are] the bait and means for spiritual fishing. . . . [The heathen Indians] are attracted more by what they receive from the missionaries, than by what is preached to them."[25]

Some Indians liked the beads that were offered. Some liked the cloth. Gifts of food were often well received. In some areas, the local inhabitants seemed fascinated by the crops that the missionaries had planted. Some, like corn, were native to Mexico but unknown in California. Others, such as wheat and barley, were native to Europe. As the rows of corn, wheat, and barley grew tall and fattened in clean straight rows, many people came to see this phenomenon.

Sometimes the biggest attraction was the drama of religious ceremony. When celebrating mass, the friars wore brightly colored ceremonial robes. They burned incense, which was swung from silver incense-burners to add a sense of smoky mystery and an exotic aroma to the air. They sipped wine from a sparkling silver chalice. The church walls were decorated with ornate religious paintings. The missionaries believed in the core values of the solemn ritual but they also knew that such display was important in evangelization. They insisted that these items of seeming luxury be among the first supplies they brought, even while they were still living in crude shelters and cooking over campfires. Palóu explained how the visitor-general had insisted that the missions be well outfitted:

The zeal of the illustrious visitor [Gálvez] was such that he wished to adorn the new missions as if they were cathedrals, for, as he said to the reverend father president, they must be beautified as much as possible, and the vestments must be the very finest, so that the heathen might see how God our Lord was worshipped, and with what care and purity the Holy Sacrifice of the Mass was said, and how the house of God our Lord was adorned, so that by this means they might be induced to embrace our Holy Faith.[26]

Physical Security

Another part of the missionaries' strategy was to offer physical security. At the College of San Fernando, missionaries had learned that providing regular hearty meals was a persuasive device for getting Indians to stay at the missions.

This was hard to do in the first years of the missions, because preparing fields and raising grains and livestock took months or years. If the friars recruited too quickly, they were unable to feed and house everyone. California's first governor, Pedro Fages, complained angrily to the viceroy in Mexico City that President Junípero Serra was irresponsible because he had allowed the missions to baptize more Indians than they were able to feed.

Within a few years crops could be harvested regularly, and livestock was raised for milk and meat. Then, the missions provided a dependable source of food. Indians found food more reliable at the missions because mission lands were irrigated to provide safeguards against California's cyclical droughts. In addition, granaries stored excess from good years to help feed residents during lean years.

Eventually many of the native Californians who moved to the missions may have

A display case at Mission San Juan Capistrano houses a silver chalice and candlesticks from the mission era. The friars used such opulent accessories to impress the Indians.

done so because they could no longer reliably feed themselves in traditional ways. Native food supplies became increasingly scarce as mission lands expanded into huge tracts for grazing for sheep and cattle or for growing wheat, corn, and other crops.

Luring Families

Another way that Indians were brought into the mission was less direct. In the early years after contact, many Indians (especially young

Water from irrigation canals flowed through this gargoyle's mouth-spout into a laundry basin.

children and the elderly) became sick from diseases common in Europe but never experienced in the Americas. Neither the friars nor traditional medicine men and women had practical remedies to cure the new diseases such as influenza, measles, chicken pox, and smallpox, but some victims recovered on their own.

In some cases, believing that a friar's prayers provided a magical cure, Indians went on their own to the missions to seek prayers and medical care. In other cases, if a person who had been baptized when he or she was seriously ill later recovered, the friars felt responsible for that person's soul and thus insisted that he or she come to live at the mission.

The friars frequently visited Indian villages to baptize sick children. When a child recovered, the friars insisted on bringing the child to live among Catholics at the mission. Usually the child's parents wanted to be near their children and thus moved the entire family to the mission.

Another strategy for getting Indians into the missions was to recruit a respected member of a tribelet, such as a chief or a shaman. Generally, when the leader accepted Catholicism, others followed. One particularly successful strategy was to recruit the leader of a tribelet that was in conflict with another. Once the leader joined, his followers would too, hoping the mission would provide protection from their rivals. In this way the missions provided a level of physical security from attacks by other native groups.

Word of Mouth

Over time, more and more Indians had seen Spanish missionaries or explorers as they crisscrossed the coastal regions and inland valleys of California. It was no longer an ex-

As later missions such as Mission San Luis Rey (pictured) were founded, recruiting became easier because the Franciscans were familiar to the native population.

traordinary event to see missionaries and soldiers with mule trains or on horses, traveling between existing missions or scouting sites for new missions.

As the missionaries seemed less foreign, recruiting became easier. When later missions were established, the friars had little trouble attracting Indians. In the first missions established in California, between 1769 and 1771, it took several years before the mission population grew beyond a hundred. When Mission San Luis Rey was founded less than thirty years later, fifty-four Indians appeared requesting baptism on the day of the founding. In 1823 several hundred Indians joined the day the last California mission was founded: San Francisco de Solano.

By the 1800s the missionaries could see that word of mouth was bringing in new converts. As Father Lasuén reported in 1803:

"Every day it is observed that, with the good treatment which they experience, the neophytes endeavor to persuade more pagans to join, and it is hoped that by this means the conversion of the rest will be effected."[27]

Spreading the Net Wider

At first the Indians who came into the mission communities were from nearby areas. However, in later years some missionaries reached out to new groups who lived at a greater distance. With the help of neophytes acting as guides and interpreters, the missionaries could travel inland from established missions and make contact with new groups.

Father Arroyo de la Cuesta was one missionary who actively searched for new recruits. He was quite good at languages. But at San

Father Arroyo de las Cuesta, who was posted at Mission San Juan Bautista (pictured), used music to communicate with new people.

Juan Bautista, the mission where he was posted, even he could not master all of the reported twenty-nine dialects and thirteen different languages spoken there. Instead, when he wanted to communicate with new people, he used music. Historian Trobridge Hall describes the technique:

> The first language of this padre was a little music box which he would load on the back of a sturdy mule, and carry to some far-away Indian settlement; there he would set it up in some prominent place and rapidly turn the crank. When the Indians first heard the strange noises they fell on their faces with fear, but as the music continued their fear left them and they began to enjoy sweet sounds, ending by slowly approaching and gathering about the padre, listening to the wonderful song box with delight. Then Padre Arroyo, just at the right moment, always turning the crank, would reload the mule

and, like the Pied Piper of Hamelin, wend his way back to the mission, all the Indians following after.[28]

In a few cases, the friars took their guard of soldiers into Indian territory and brought new Indians back to a mission by force. Such action was contrary to Franciscan missionary policy but it did happen occasionally.

Joining the Church: Baptism

The friars' first step in saving souls was to make the Indians aware of the friars, the missions, and basic concepts of Catholicism. The second step was to baptize those who wished to join the church.

For the friars, baptism was the beginning of a person's spiritual life, cleansing the soul of any previous sins. Each baptism was a sacred event and the cause of considerable celebration. Friars were delighted when a person was baptized, as this meant that one more soul had been saved.

The person being baptized was supposed to do so willingly. Usually an Indian needed to have gained a basic understanding and acceptance of Christianity before he could request baptism. In the experience of the missionaries, it took most adults about three months of instruction before they had learned sufficiently about Catholicism to request to be baptized and received into the church.

Mission Life as a Lifelong Vow

The friars assumed that all Indians who were baptized should live permanently at the mission. Just as the friars had taken permanent vows when they completed their novitiate and joined the Franciscan order, they believed that Indians who were baptized had joined the Christian community. As French visitor La Pérouse explained:

It must be observed that the moment an Indian is baptized, the effect is the same as if he had pronounced a vow for life. If he escapes to reside with his relations in the independent villages, he is summoned three times to return; if he refuses, the missionaries apply to the governor, who sends soldiers to him in the midst of his family and conduct him to the mission, where he is condemned to receive a certain number of lashes with the whip. As these people are at war with their neighbors, they can never escape to a distance greater than twenty or thirty leagues.[29]

Baptizing an Old Cacique

Spaniard José Cardero, as published in Donald C. Cutter's *California in 1792,* told the story about how one cacique, or Indian leader, came to be baptized on his deathbed:

"The leader of one of these pagan tribes, as respected for his valor as he was loved by his people for the natural talents he possessed, was at death's door. He had shown esteem for the father president, and I don't know whether or not he had done him some kindness. When the latter learned of the sad situation of the former on a stormy night of constant rain, despite his dwelling place being some leagues away, he went there for the purpose of persuading him not to depart his world without embracing the Catholic faith and purifying himself with holy baptism. After great difficulty he arrived at last to talk with him, and having made known to him the reason for his trip and of the ardent desire that he had that a person whom he loved would not be lost forever, but rather, by trying to persuade him to the truth of what he was telling him and subjecting him to the ceremonies required by Christianity, he would obtain the reward that is promised to those who duly profess it. Then the pagan, being convinced, said to the father president: 'I believe what you tell me and I will do what you direct because I find that no other interest but what you tell me can have motivated you to leave the comforts of your home to travel a number of leagues on a stormy night; I am convinced of your good will and I place myself in your hands.'"

San Diego Slow to Baptize

The San Diego mission had more troubles than most. In his *Historical Memoirs,* Francisco Palóu reported sadly that six months after its founding,

"Such was the state of the mission on the 24th of January, 1770. . . . It had not baptized a single [person] for, although the fathers did everything possible to convert them and had induced the parents of a little girl to give their consent that she be baptized and to be present at the ceremony of baptism in the chapel, when the reverend father president was about to pour the holy water on her the heathen snatched her away and ran off with her, leaving the father chagrined."

Sometimes neophytes were allowed to leave the mission for a few days or a week at a time, either to visit their ancestral homes or to collect native foods that were in season. They might fish the rivers, ocean, or tide pools; they might gather acorns, pine nuts, or grasses; or they might hunt deer and other game. Leave to search for food was most common in the early mission days, before the mission farms were productive enough to feed everyone.

At the end of their time away most neophytes returned as scheduled. However, some chose not to return. Of the neophytes who were baptized, as many as one in ten did not stay at the mission throughout their life.

Neophytes explained their escapes and other unauthorized absences in various ways. Some worried that mission life was unhealthy. Some wanted to go "home" to die, so that they could be with the spirits of their ancestors. Others said they felt lonely or homesick and wanted to be with their relatives. Many complained that they had to work too hard at the mission, or that they had been punished too harshly.

Mission Culture Everywhere

The native people had not invited the missionaries to come to California. The missionaries came anyway, fervently believing that they could bring Christianity to California and save the souls of countless natives there. Within the few decades that the missions prospered, the missionaries had achieved much of what they had come for. Most native villages had been replaced by mission settlements. Nearly all Indians spoke Spanish and had been baptized Catholic. During this period the people and way of life in California had changed dramatically.

CHAPTER 4

Daily Life of the Mission Indians

A mission provided food, housing, and religious support for the neophytes. In return, the neophytes were expected to stay at the mission and live a regimented life devoted primarily to work and spiritual growth. This was a life the friars believed would transform native Californians into good Catholics.

A worker rings a bell summoning a mission community to sunrise mass.

Daily Schedule

From sunrise until early evening the Indians' time was filled with work and prayer. One visitor showed particular interest in the meals that broke up other daily activities. This visitor, the French nobleman Jean-François de Galoup de La Pérouse, was the commanding officer of two French ships that called at Monterey Bay in 1786. In his journal, he described a typical day at the nearby Carmel mission:

> The Indians as well as the missionaries rise with the sun, and immediately go to prayers and mass, which last for an hour. During this time three large boilers are set on the fire for cooking a kind of soup, made of bar-ley meal, the grain of which has been roasted previous to its being ground. This sort of food, of which the Indians are extremely fond, is called *atole*. They eat it without either butter or salt, a most insipid mess.
>
> Each hut sends for [its] allowance of [soup for] all its inhabitants in a vessel made of the bark of a tree. There is neither confusion nor disorder in the distribution, and when the boilers are nearly emptied, the thicker portion at the bottom is distributed to those children who have said their catechism the best.
>
> The time of repast is three quarters of an hour, after which they all go to work, some to till the ground with oxen, some

Most activities at a mission were performed in response to the tolling of bells, which signaled such daily events as the time to rise, to attend church, to eat, and to retire.

Supplementing Mission Meals

Several eyewitnesses described how neophytes supplemented the meals prepared for everyone at the missions with traditional native foods, including grasses, seeds, and game. Donald C. Cutter, in *California in 1792,* includes José Cardero's description of what he saw at the mission in Carmel, in 1792:

"Those who are in the mission have not yet lost fondness for such [native] foods, for we have seen a girl chew with considerable pleasure stalks of the most tasteless plants; and despite being aided by those provided by the mission, they gather a great quantity of the seeds to which they are accustomed. . . . To eat those that they use in place of bread, they toast them in trays by throwing heated stones over the seeds and mixing these with them until they get them to the proper point. Then they grind them in wooden mortars, very well made by them; and now that they have instruments with which to do it easily and know the advantage, they boil them and leave them to form pap. . . .

[For] hunting deer, . . . they keep the skins of some heads of these animals with their horns and part of the neck, and skinned with much care. . . . On going out to hunt, they fit these caps over their heads, and situated in a convenient place, they stand on three 'feet,' including the left hand. With the right hand they have their bow and arrow ready, and as soon as they see one of those animals, they note whether it is male or female, and . . . try to imitate the movements appropriate to the opposite sex, which they do with perfect similarity that, by attracting it within range, they fire the arrow that rarely fails to have the sought-after effect."

to dig in the garden, while others are employed in domestic occupations, all under the eye of one or two missionaries.

At noon the bells give notice of the time of dinner. The Indians then quit their work, and send for their allowance in the same vessel as at breakfast. But this second soup is thicker than the former, and contains a mixture of wheat, maize, peas, and beans; the Indians call it *pozole.*

They return to work from two to four or five o'clock, when they repair to evening prayer, which lasts nearly an hour and is followed by a distribution of *atole,* the same as at breakfast. These three distributions are sufficient for the subsistence of the greater number of these Indians.[30]

Mission bells rang throughout the day to mark regular times for waking, attending church, working, eating meals, relaxing, and sleeping. Bells also rang at unscheduled hours to call attention to special events such as the arrival of visitors or feast day activities.

A Day's Work

Work occupied much of everyone's time at the mission. Six days a week they worked in the fields or at a trade. The seventh was a day of rest and prayer. Friars believed that hard work made a person virtuous.

Neophytes worked regularly for other reasons too. As much as possible, the missions produced everything they needed to survive. The food they raised was shared among everyone at the mission, including those who worked at other tasks and those who were too young, too old, or too sick to work. When the neophytes at one mission produced a surplus, it was shared with other missions or bartered in exchange for other items needed at the mission. In 1792 Spanish eyewitness José Cardero explained the sharing and lack of individual ownership this way:

> Up to now it has been customary in the missions to oblige all the Indians to work for everyone, without permitting property to anyone, both because this system has seemed more suitable to the brotherhood and union that should reign in a small society and because they had experienced that those to whom a plot of ground had been assigned [individually] cared very little for its cultivation, if not abandoning it altogether.[31]

Farming

More neophytes worked in agriculture than anything else. Men plowed the fields and

A museum in the original grain storage area at Mission San Juan Capistrano displays typical foods and storage vessels of the mission era.

Organizing Work

The neophyte, Pablo Tac, left San Luis Rey Mission at the age of ten. His knowledge of mission life is a combination of his own experiences and stories told by friars. In *Indian Life and Customs,* Tac explained how neophytes were organized to do work at Mission San Luis Rey.

"The [friar], as he was alone and . . . seeing that it would be very difficult for him alone to give orders to that people, and, moreover, people that had left the woods just a few years before, therefore appointed alcaldes from the people themselves that knew how to speak Spanish more than the others and were better than the others in their customs. There were seven alcaldes, with rods as a symbol that they could judge the others. . . . The chief of the alcaldes was called the general. He knew the name of each one. . . . In the afternoon, the alcaldes gather at the house of the missionary. They bring the news of that day."

planted and harvested crops. Boys helped with light tasks such as weeding or scaring birds and other animals away from the fields. Women and girls helped when all hands were needed, especially during the planting season and at harvest.

As many as a thousand or more people lived together at a mission. They could not be fed using the traditional native way of finding food by hunting for small game, fishing, and foraging for acorns and other wild plant products. Neophytes learned to farm in order to produce enough food for the entire community. In mission fields and gardens they cultivated wheat, corn, barley, beans, peas, chickpeas, tomatoes, and many kinds of fruit including dates, pomegranates, oranges, lemons, peaches,

apples, pears, grapes, and other Mexican and European crops.

To prepare the fields for planting, neophytes used a primitive plow. A pair of oxen pulled the plow across the fields. This plow was no match for tough soils, and they had to crisscross each field many times. Once the topsoil was turned over and the grounds prepared, Indian women and children scattered seeds. Then, others dragged tree branches over the rows to cover the seeds.

At harvest time almost everybody living at the mission went to the fields to help bring in the year's crop. They cut the stalks of wheat or barley and then loaded them into the carts, called *carretas*, to haul them back to the mission. At the mission they placed

As the herds of mission livestock grew, they were usually moved to unfenced ranches some distance from the mission grounds.

the stalks on a hard earthen or tiled floor in an enclosed space. There, mules or oxen were driven over the stalks so that their hooves loosened the edible grains from the stalks. Indian women tossed what was left into the air, sifting it to catch the grain in baskets and let the wind blow away the rest. This process is called winnowing. Grains were stored in the granaries inside the mission buildings.

Ten years after the founding of Mission Santa Barbara, the missionaries' year-end report explains that they sometimes still needed to rely on supplies from other missions:

> We are dependent upon the rain, because the running water of the mission is not abundant [especially in] July, August, and September. . . . The harvests are small considering the amount of grain planted. . . . For the year 1794 we planted 98 fanegas of wheat, 2 1/2 fanegas of corn; but only 15 fanegas of corn were realized, and of the wheat only 400 fanegas. Foreseeing that there would be a lack of provisions until the year 1795, we had recourse to the Missions of Purísima Concepción and San Luís Obispo, and their Rev. Missionaries supplied our neophytes with 250 fanegas of wheat and corn.[32]

Ranching

All missions raised large herds of cattle and sheep and some goats, mules, and horses. In the early days the livestock was kept right at the missions. Neophytes built fences of lashed poles or cacti planted close to each other to keep the animals from stomping through the planted fields. Young boys took turns shooing the livestock away from areas where they should not be.

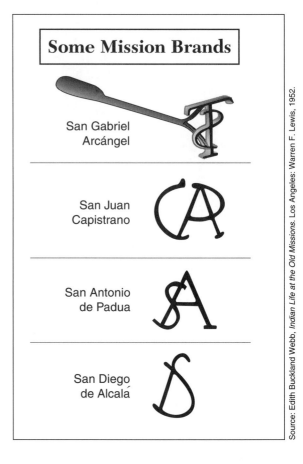

Some Mission Brands

San Gabriel Arcángel

San Juan Capistrano

San Antonio de Padua

San Diego de Alcalá

Source: Edith Buckland Webb, *Indian Life at the Old Missions*. Los Angeles: Warren F. Lewis, 1952.

As the herds grew, the animals were moved to pastures farther away from the mission buildings. Some ranches were a one- or two-day ride from the main area of the mission. The ranches were unfenced, and the herds often ran semiwild.

Each year neophyte cowboys rounded up the livestock to be counted. The calves and other young animals born that year were marked with the special brand developed for each mission.

Each mission had its own distinctive brand. Once a year mission livestock was rounded up. Young animals, who were still with their mothers, were branded so that they could not be confused with animals of other missions or ranches. Branding cattle was important because as the number of livestock grew and ranged across more land, one mission's herd often mixed with herds from other missions and from private Spanish ranches. The brand burned into an animal's hide was the only way to distinguish one from another.

The scientist Georg H. von Langsdorff, who traveled on a Russian ship to California in 1806, described what he saw when he visited the San Francisco bay area missions in 1806:

> The cattle, horses, and sheep do not require any particular attention. The herds are left in the open the whole year through. Only a sufficient number are kept in the neighborhood of the establishment to serve immediate wants. When a supply of cattle is wanted, some of the neophytes and soldiers are sent out to the pastures, on horseback, and with riatas [lassos], which they throw very dexterously, catch by the horns the number required.[33]

Home on the Range

Riding a horse gave a person both freedom and power. For fear of letting the friars lose control of native Californians, Spanish law did not permit Indians to ride horses except under unusual circumstances. The duties of a cowboy were considered unusual, and allowed for a few trusted Indians to ride horseback.

When cowboys and others needed to live permanently at pastures and ranches that were at some distance from the mission center, neophytes built a chapel and housing at these outposts. Twenty such settlements, called *asistencias* or sub-missions were eventually built in California. They provided semipermanent living quarters for neophytes in ranching. Friars visited the *asistencias* to perform church services. When men lived away from the mission grounds, their wives often went along to cook, collect firewood, and provide other support.

Working in Construction

Many men worked in construction during the long periods when the missions were being built and rebuilt. The friars, and sometimes outside experts, created the design and managed construction, but the neophytes provided the manual labor. A few neophytes at every mission were also taught skilled building trades including carpentry, stone masonry, and blacksmithing.

Neophytes also learned to make all the building materials needed, as none could be imported. They learned to saw tree trunks to make them into usable lumber. With large two-man saws, they transformed logs into flat planks and beams to support the roofs. To make adobe bricks, they mixed local clay with straw and sometimes horse manure, and forced the mixture into wooden forms to dry in the sun. When dry, an adobe brick weighed about sixty pounds. They used a different mixture of clay to form flat floor tiles and curved roof tiles, which were baked until they became very hard in a special oven called a kiln. They ground seashells into powder, which they burned to make lime for plastering walls. They also dug, cut, and carried blocks of stone from rock quarries to the missions. Even nails were created by California blacksmiths.

When new buildings were underway, women helped by carrying the adobe bricks and tiles from the drying fields and kilns to the carts for transport. Older women and children helped out by collecting firewood for the kilns.

Frenchman Auguste Duhaut-Cilly visited Mission Santa Barbara in 1827. He watched

The Indian Fernando Librado was born on one of the Channel Islands off the coast of Santa Barbara sometime in the early 1800s. As a toddler, he moved with his family to Mission San Buenaventura, where he was baptized and lived until the end of the mission period. An anthropologist from the Smithsonian Institution conducted a series of interviews with Librado between 1912 and 1915.

His recollections of Mission San Buenaventura, as recorded in Travis Hudson's *Breath of the Sun: Life in Early California As Told by a Chumash Indian, Fernando Librado to John P. Harrington*, include this description of construction with adobe bricks.

"The Indians brought the water for making the adobes in containers suspended from poles which were carried across their shoulders. . . . Those that laid the adobe bricks were called adoberos. Juan Pedro Abañil, a Ventura Indian, was one of these. His Indian name was Timiyahaut, which means 'the powder.' This referred to the dust or powder which the coyote scratches up with his four feet when he is contented. It is a name in the old mystic language.

Another adobero was Laveriano Toponxele, whose Indian nickname meant 'a classy intruder.' Laveriano always managed to intrude with pomp. He was my godfather at my first confirmation. Once Juan Pedro Abañil and Laveriano were laying adobes at Mission San Buenaventura. Juan was on top giving directions. He would call

from above, counting the number of bricks that he needed by tens. He used a kind of grunt each time he counted ten, and he would also close his hands and bring them down from his shoulders to his hips, saying 'toi,' meaning ten. The fifth time he would say 'yitipake'es k'ik'wi.' There were other grunted words for the tens but I cannot remember them."

Adobe bricks dry in the sun just as they did during the mission period.

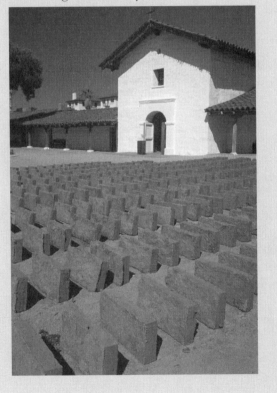

the neophytes at work and described their labors.

Out of raw earth he had to make bricks and tile; he had to fell great trees at a distance and transport them by physical effort over new roads built past ravines and precipices; to gather from the shore and with great effort seashells for the making of lime; in sum, even the smallest elements of the building cost much preliminary work, thus adding greatly to the difficulties.[34]

Under the direction of outside engineers or mission friars, neophytes also created sophisticated long-distance irrigation systems by rerouting water from streams and rivers into the mission grounds. Sometimes water was channeled through miles of tile-lined ditches and aqueducts to be stored in reservoirs outside the mission quadrangle. From there, water could be piped into fountains where neophytes took what they needed for cooking and drinking. From the fountains it flowed to the wide basins of the laundry areas, where neophyte women scrubbed the clothes clean. Water that ran off from the laundry basins was allowed to settle again to separate out the soap, then it was diverted into the fields to irrigate crops and water livestock.

Other Mission Labor

For those who did not work in farming or ranching, there were other tasks to do. Neophytes might be given jobs preparing meals, spinning wool, weaving cloth, making tiles and adobe bricks, and processing goods for use at the missions or for trade.

A few women were responsible for preparing the *atole* and *pozole* that everyone ate for breakfast, dinner, and supper. As La Pérouse describes, roasting and grinding corn and other grains for these meals was difficult and required special skill:

Frenchman La Pérouse presented the Carmel mission with a "modern" gristmill like the one pictured here. The mill was an improvement over the traditional method of laboriously grinding corn by hand.

Grinding of corn . . . is both tedious and laborious, because they have no other method of breaking the grain than with a roller upon a stone. . . .

The whole art of this cookery consists in roasting the grain before it is reduced to meal. As the Indian women have no clay or metallic vessels for this operation, they perform it in baskets of bark by using small burning wood coals. They turn these vessels with such dexterity and rapidity that they succeed in causing the grain to swell and burst without burning the basket, though made of combustible material.[35]

Cattle were slaughtered weekly for food and other purposes. Mission residents were able to use nearly every part of the animal. In addition to eating the meat, they boiled beef fat in large kettles to make tallow. Tallow was made into candles and also refined into soap. Some of the mission Indians skinned the carcasses of slaughtered cattle. Others scraped the hides clean, tanned them, and stretched them in the sun to dry. Some rawhides were used for bedding or sold. At a few missions, the men turned the rawhides into fine leather. The leather was made into boots, saddles, and other goods.

Once a year, sheep were shorn of their wool. Women and girls cleaned and carded the wool, then spun it into yarn. Either men or women used the mission's looms to weave the yarn into rough blankets and cloth.

Spinning, weaving, and making bricks and tiles occupied many hours each week. These jobs were done on a piecework basis, meaning neophytes who produced these crafts were required to produce a certain amount of cloth or tiles every week. Father Estévan Tápis of the Santa Barbara mission

Mission San Juan Capistrano has preserved these huge mission-era vessels used for making tallow, a substance fashioned into candles and refined into soap.

Odd Jobs Around the Mission

Travis Hudson's *Breath of the Sun* includes Fernando Librado's memories of life at Mission San Buenaventura, and of how old men often worked cleaning up around the mission. Librado, a Native Californian, lived at the mission nearly his whole life.

"At Mission San Buenaventura . . . there were the sweepers. It was the obligation for old men to bring brooms every Saturday. Some of these brooms were for the [dormitory], some were for the . . . kitchen, the church, the padres' rooms, the wine cellar, and for the loom room. The [weaving] room required four brooms alone. These various brooms were made of Juncus [rush] and used for fine sweeping.

For outside use the sweepers did not use the Juncus brooms. These non-Juncus brooms were needed for cleaning out the baking ovens, as well as for sweeping the plazas. There were two fountains south of the present church at Mission San Buenaventura, and in a little plaza there the sweepers would pile the dirt. This pile was later picked up by an ox cart and hauled away."

described the work entailed in making adobe bricks and tiles:

Men make the adobes. Nine men will make three hundred and sixty adobes a day, which is forty for each one. The soil is soft and the water is near by. Those who work at this task never labor after eleven o'clock in the morning, and never on Saturdays, nor many times on Fridays, because during the first days of the week they have accomplished the task for the last days, and are then free. Those who make tiles have a certain number to make. Sixteen young men, and at times as many more middle-aged men, with two women who bring the sand and straw, make 500 tiles a day. The troughs with the clay are close by and are always filled.[36]

Everyone Worked

Mission children were expected to work beside the grown-ups, helping where they could and learning the skills they would use through-out their lives. Some children had special jobs. A few boys were taught to ring the mission bells. Those with promising voices were taught to sing in the choir. A few boys served the friars directly, either as servants or as altar boys who helped during church services.

The elderly and disabled continued to be part of the mission community. Those who could, worked at jobs that were less strenuous. For example, old women frequently spent their days collecting firewood. At one mission, a blind neophyte worked reciting religious lessons to the newer converts. Those who were no longer able to work still lived at the mission, where they continued to receive free food, housing, and medical care.

Home Life

Neophyte families lived in houses clustered just outside the walls of the mission quadrangle. In the early years these houses were built in traditional native style: temporary structures of branches covered with reeds and grasses. At some missions these simple houses

Photographed in the 1860s, California Indians stand outside their one-room adobe house. The sturdy dwelling was an improvement over the more simple, grass-covered structures in which California natives once lived.

were eventually replaced with more permanent adobe structures lined up in rows. These adobe houses each had a single room, about ten feet wide by fifteen feet long, with one door and one window.

Narrow lanes separated the rows of houses and led to the gardens where the Indian women grew fruits and vegetables, and where they raised chickens and other small animals for food. Sometimes a fire pit was set inside the house, sometimes it was outside the walls. There was no running water in the houses. The Indians brought water from the central fountain to their houses in baskets or gourds.

Within their homes neophyte families created their own culture, which mixed the ways of the friars with many of the practices of their ancestors. For example, they continued to speak their mother tongue. They supplemented mission meals with traditional foods—

acorns, grasses, pine nuts, wild game, and fish—which were stored and prepared using traditional methods. They also crafted and played with traditional toys and musical instruments such as flutes, whistles, and drums.

Growing Up at the Mission

The typical mission family included a married couple and their young children. Marriage was a lifelong commitment; divorce was not recognized or allowed. Older people did not live with their children and grandchildren. They lived in their own houses.

From the age of eight or nine, children lived apart from their families. It was mission policy to separate the children from their parents so the younger generation could be more easily taught to be good Catholics.

Girls were the most isolated group at a mission. They lived, worked, ate, and slept in a special part of the mission called the *monjerío,* literally, the nuns' quarters. During the mission era a common European belief was that unmarried girls must be kept safe both from worldly temptations and from all boys and men. In fact, single neophyte women of all ages lived at the *monjerío.* If a woman's husband died, she was compelled by mission policy to return to live at the *monjerío.*

A *monjerío* had its own sleeping quarters (sometimes on a loft above the work area), workshops, kitchen, toilet facilities, and often its own small courtyard with a fountain, laundry, and garden. The *monjerío* was usually located at the back corner of a mission compound, surrounded by the walls of the mission quadrangle. It had only one door, which led to an inner courtyard and could easily be guarded. Its only windows were placed high above the ground to provide light and air but also to prevent anyone sneaking in or out.

Every night the door to the *monjerío* was locked, and the key was given to a trusted female guardian or one of the missionaries for safekeeping. Christian women (often the wives or widows of soldiers) who lived at the mission sometimes acted as chaperones when the girls left the *monjerío* to go to church or visit their families in the mission village.

Before the mission period, women and girls had spent much of their time gathering food as they wandered through the lands surrounding their village. Now their lives were confined to the *monjerío.* At some missions, in the morning or afternoon after they had finished their work, the girls were allowed

Dress and Clothing

Dress varied from mission to mission and season to season. At first, neophytes often wore the same kind of clothing they had worn before mission times. Published in Donald C. Cutter, *California in 1792,* Spaniard José Cardero described what he saw in Monterey in 1792:

"The men, with the exception of those employed in the principal occupations such as majordomo, sacristan, blacksmith, carpenter, and so on, go around undressed in summer, with nothing more than modesty indispensably requires. The Indian women have tied to their waists a fringe made of palm leaves or dry grass that reaches their knees, and over the shoulders a cape of coarse cloth or of sea otter skins with which they cover their bodies to the knees."

As time went on, more of the neophytes wore clothing of European style. The fabric was woven from the wool shorn from mission sheep. Sometimes the fabric was colored using natural plant dyes but usually it was the color of the sheep: a combination of blacks, whites, and browns. Neophyte women cut and sewed the cloth to make clothing.

Clothing and blankets were distributed twice a year. Each person got one blanket and one outfit. If an article tore or was worn out before the end of the year, they could request a replacement.

Women and girls wore a blouse and skirt. Men and boys wore a shirt and breechcloth. When they were cold they wrapped themselves in their blankets, which were also woven at the missions. Cowboys were given extra clothing, appropriate to life on a ranch: boots, a hat, leggings, and a poncho.

out to visit their parents. Only when they married were young women allowed to leave the *monjerío* permanently.

Boys lived a much freer life than their sisters. They slept in a large communal dormitory but they were not locked in. When they were not in school, in church, or helping with work, boys could wander anywhere they wanted at the mission.

The friars encouraged teenaged boys and girls to marry. However, there was no courtship or dating. Boys and girls might catch a glimpse of each other across the church or in the courtyard but they were forbidden to meet, let alone talk or get to know each other. Usually a boy asked the friar to arrange his marriage to a particular girl. Then the friar asked the girl if she was interested. If everyone agreed, the couple was married in three weeks and then were assigned their own house in the neophyte village. If the girl did not agree, the boy chose someone else.

School Days

There was no separate school building at the mission, but boys and girls were still expected to study and learn. At specified times during the day, while adults were working, one of the friars or a well-educated neophyte taught the children their lessons. At some missions, the girls and boys studied together. At others, the girls took their lessons separately inside the *monjerío*.

As they grew up, children learned many practical skills (such as how to farm, cook, weave, and tend animals) but these skills they

Young Native American girls in California learn basket weaving, just as their mission forebears once did.

Cats and Dogs

As early as 1776, the friars asked that cats be sent to California because rats and other rodents were eating the food stored in the granaries and the crops in the fields. At the missions the cats roamed freely. Holes were cut in the bottom of wooden church doors so that the cats could chase after mice even when the doors were closed to people.

Dogs were also active participants in mission life. Some dogs were native to California, others were brought with the Spanish. They were active helpers, working as shepherds for the livestock and as scarecrows in the farming fields. A number of dogs served as companions around the missions.

learned "on the job," working next to the adults. In class they learned to speak Spanish, recite prayers, and memorize the catechism, or teachings of Christianity. Few Indian children were taught to read and write or do arithmetic, because the friars did not believe these skills would help them in their daily lives.

Leisure Time

In the evening after supper, the Indians were free to relax. At most missions the favorite gathering place was the *pozolera* (the dining room). Here boys, single men, and married couples could play instruments, sing, dance, or relax over a game of skill or chance. The girls were confined to the *monjerío* but everyone else could come and go as they pleased. Some of the neophytes played the instruments they had learned to play in church, including drums, flutes, and string instruments such as the violin, viola, and guitar. However, evening entertainment frequently consisted of traditional Indian songs, dance, and games.

Feast days provided the perfect opportunity to break the strict daily routine of church service and work. Each mission celebrated special feast days at various times throughout the year. These celebrations were designed both to reinforce Christian teachings and to lessen the boredom of everyday life. The important celebrations lasted several days. Frenchman Auguste Duhaut-Cilly, who arrived at Mission San Luis Rey just before the feast day of San Antonio in 1827, described what he heard and saw:

> The mission was all astir with preparations for the two festivals. . . . Although these were religious occasions, the superior of the mission, wishing to attract the greatest number of people, was accustomed to keep open house and to provide all the spectacles, games, and amusements so dear to the Californians . . . [including] a high mass chanted by Indian musicians. . . . Immediately after mass came the bullfights, which lasted for much of the day.[37]

Staying Healthy, Succumbing to Disease

At a mission, like in any town of its size, sometimes people got sick or died. However, the number of sick and dying was higher than would be expected in a town this size for several reasons.

The most significant reason for high death rates was that the Spanish had unwittingly introduced new diseases against which the Indian population had no immunity. Native Californians had never been exposed to illnesses that had become common in Europe. These included influenza, measles, chicken pox, and smallpox. When germs from any of these ailments spread to the indigenous population, many people died.

Also, while the Spanish population at the missions were all adults, neophytes were of all ages: infants, toddlers, young, and old. Young children and old people are generally the groups most likely to get sick. To make matters worse, because everyone lived so close to each other at a mission, contagious diseases spread rapidly.

In the thirty-four years between 1769, the time the first mission was founded, and 1803, just over half of all those who had been baptized had died. Nearly all the deaths were due to disease, not violence. Of course, some had died of old age, but many of those who died were infants, children, and young adults. Yet when the friars first arrived in California, the native population was quite healthy.

So much illness and death among the Indians also helped undermine their faith in traditional healers. Their healing practices and remedies were no match for the germs unwittingly transferred from the Europeans. Traditionally, native Californian men strengthened and purified themselves in sweat houses called *temescals*. While the intense heat of the *temescal* was the right solution for cleansing a healthy body, it aggravated the symptoms of the newly introduced diseases such as measles, smallpox, and chicken pox, and left the Indians even sicker.

The friars and government officials were concerned about the high death rates among the neophytes. Periodically, they requested special reports about how the neophytes were being treated, how much they worked, and their living conditions. They also sent government physicians to investigate the health problems. The only conclusions they could draw were that the Indians bathed too frequently and did not protect themselves from drafty airs. At Santa Barbara mission, Father Estévan Tápis explained,

Temescals

In pre-mission California, Indian men used sweat houses, called *temescals*, to stay healthy and as meeting rooms. There was a *temescal* in most villages. Donald C. Cutter, in *California in 1792*, includes Spanish eyewitness José Cardero's 1792 description:

"These natives make a circular trench in the ground and then they cover it with a bell-shaped hood, leaving a very narrow door as an entrance to that room, making it an oven. On one side of it they throw some firewood which they burn at the proper time. When the men come in from work, they go off to that heater, which is already prepared with the proper fire. They enter gradually up to the number that it can hold, while those who have to wait amuse themselves with various games.

Those who are inside suffer that unnatural heat that there is inside the heat chamber until they sweat a great deal; when they leave, they scrape their skin with the edge of a shell for that purpose, taking off with the sweat the filth that covers them. Afterwards they bathe in the river and on coming out they wallow in the dirt."

We missionary Fathers are careful, as far as possible, that the Mission lacks nothing in the way of medicines, very frequently needed for ourselves as well as for the neophytes. Besides these medicines, other methods of curing ills are in vogue. The most common are purging oneself with sea water; bathing in sea water, and in . . . the warm waters that are in the vicinity of the Mission; and applying injections. These medical treatments are the most common among the Indians and the least dangerous, considering what little care they take of themselves, and how frequently, when taking some medicine, they are told to avoid being in a draft, or getting wet, or exposing their health to other dangers. The infirmities among these Indians are the same that are common to all men.[38]

Discipline

Neophytes were taught to understand the difference between right and wrong as part of their training in Catholicism. If they misbehaved, they were expected to accept their punishment. In Europe at this time, corporal punishment (whipping, flogging, shackles, and so on) was common, and so it was at the missions.

Neophytes who were caught talking in church were scolded. Those who did not work hard enough could be whipped. At some missions the most common infraction was trying to escape or not returning after an authorized leave. Estévan Tápis, in his 1800 report, described how Santa Barbara mission neophytes were punished for wrongdoing.

[When] a man, a boy, or a woman, runs away or does not return from the excur-

Whipping was a common punishment in Europe (pictured here in England), and the practice was applied to neophytes guilty of laziness or trying to escape from the mission.

sion, other neophytes must be sent after them. When such a one is brought back to the Mission, he is reproached for not having heard holy Mass on a day of obligation. He is made to see that he has of his own free will taken upon himself this and other Christian duties, and he is warned that he will be chastised if he repeats the transgression. He runs away again, and again he is brought back. This time he is chastised with the lash or with the stocks. If this is not sufficient, as is the case with some who disregard a warning, he is made to feel the shackles, which he must wear three days while at work. . . .

Those who steal something of value or who engage in a dangerous fight . . . are first chastised and then made to abhor theft or exhorted to preserve peace.

There is no jail [except] the pozolera [which] . . . is open day and night and is always visited by the Indians; but the stocks are there, which is the most common punishment. . . . As a rule, the women are punished with one, two, or three days in the stocks [located in the monjerío], according to the gravity of the offense. If the delinquents prove obstinate in their evil or if they run away, they are chastised in the [monjerío] by the hand of another woman.[39]

A New Way of Life

During the mission period the way of life for native Californians was changed dramatically. They learned to live in settled, farming communities and to pray to the Christian god. They were subjects of the Spanish Crown but they never became full Spanish citizens.

CHAPTER 5
Daily Life of the Friars

According to Antonio María de Bucareli, the viceroy of New Spain in 1773, the missionaries had "the right to manage the mission Indians as a father would manage his family."[40]

To the friars, a mission was far more than the complex of buildings—it was a family of native Californians living as Christians. The friars followed their own religious path while guiding the larger community in both religious and practical matters.

Daily Devotions

The missions were thousands of miles from the College of San Fernando in Mexico City, and farther still from the friars' homes in Spain. Here, among the Indians, the friars lived as Franciscans with the same structured discipline they had learned during the novitiate. Their schedule of prayer, work, meals, and rest varied little from day to day.

As many as seven times a day the friars attended chapel to celebrate mass or to pray for the needs of the Indians, themselves, the Franciscan order, and the church as a whole. These services helped remind them of their purpose as Franciscans and as missionaries.

The daily religious rigors started some time between midnight and 2 A.M. The most zealous friars woke then and walked to the chapel to conduct the set of prayers called matins. (Some friars followed the accepted practice of celebrating matins before they went to sleep at night, thus allowing themselves to get sufficient rest for the hard work that faced them the next day.) They all rose at dawn and prayed privately before ringing the bells to call the entire community to the church to celebrate morning mass.

The friars were back in church at noon, and again in the mid-afternoon, when they continued their private daily prayer sessions. About 5 or 6 P.M. the bells rang again to call everyone to join them in the church. After the Indians left, the friars celebrated vespers, an evening service. One last time, at about 9 P.M., the friars returned to the chapel to say their night prayers just before retiring.

Providing Spiritual Leadership and Guidance

The friars led busy lives. When they were not in church attending to their personal religious duties, the friars were actively involved in both the spiritual and working lives of the larger mission community.

Friars celebrated mass and other daily services as well as the services for special holy days (such as Lent, Easter, Advent, Christmas). In addition, they baptized babies, performed marriages of young men and women, and last rites for the sick and dying.

In the early days, when mission sites were being scouted, missionaries accompanied the soldiers on their exploratory ventures. Once a mission was founded, the friars

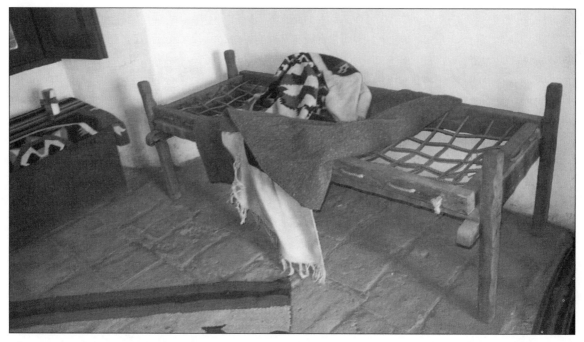

The most zealous friars rose from their uncomfortable beds as early as midnight to celebrate the prayers known as matins. *Mission San Juan Capistrano displays the mission bed replica pictured here.*

encouraged Indians to approach and join the community. It was a friar's duty to recruit new converts and to provide basic religious education prior to baptism.

Daily Instruction

Every day of the year the friars worked with the neophytes, teaching them the fundamentals of Roman Catholicism. The friars needed to build on the rudimentary knowledge adult neophytes had acquired before baptism. Everyone at the mission received additional religious instruction during morning and afternoon church services.

Sometimes the friars trained one neophyte to tutor the others in the ways of Catholicism in their own language. Such a tutor allowed the friars to spend time working at other tasks without abandoning their

students. English visitor Frederick William Beechey described a class that he saw at one of the missions in 1826:

> They [the neophytes] were clothed in blankets and arranged in a row before a blind Indian, who understood their dialect and was assisted by an *alcalde* [an Indian leader] to keep order. Their tutor began by desiring them to kneel, informing them that he was going to teach them the names of the Persons composing the Trinity, and that they were to repeat in Spanish what he dictated.
>
> The neophytes being thus arranged, the speaker began: "*Santisima Trinidad, Dios, Jesu Christo, Espirito Santo,*" [Holy Trinity, God, Jesus Christ, Holy Ghost]—pausing between each name to listen if the simple Indians, who had never

spoken a Spanish word before, pronounced it correctly . . . After they had repeated these names satisfactorily, their blind tutor, after a pause added *"Santos"* [Saints] and recapitulated the names of a great many saints, which finished the morning's [instruction].[41]

Teaching Through Art and Music

The friars struggled to find ways to teach Christianity to the Indians and to give them daily spiritual inspiration. Art and music were two of the most effective tools for teaching the neophytes about Christianity.

The friars used music to teach Catholic rituals and also to help make church services more appealing. Music played an integral part in both lessons and church ceremonies. Each day during church services the friars sang a few basic hymns. By repeating them every day, everyone soon learned to sing along. Also, several parts of the ceremony were presented musically in a statement-response format. That is, the friar or a musically gifted assistant chanted part of a prayer, and the congregation replied by chanting a standard response.

Most missions incorporated a choir into church services. Boys and men who had good voices were invited to sing in the choir. (The friars were supposed to avoid all direct contact with women, so women and girls were excluded from the choir.) Several missions also had large orchestras with many kinds of instruments including organs, violins, violas, basses, piccolos, flutes, oboes, clarinets, trumpets, horns, triangles, and several drums. Instruments such as flutes and violins were often used to keep the melody for the singing, and drums kept the beat.

Architecture, painting, and sculpture were also central to religious life and training

Teaching the Catechism

In his journal, Spanish eyewitness José Cardero included his impressions of his visit to the mission at Carmel in 1792. He also copied into the journal a trilingual dictionary that the local friars had compiled. It translates between Spanish and the two major native languages in the Carmel valley, Runsien and Eslen. The dictionary includes numbers from one to thirty and such common terms as man, woman, son, daughter, sea otter, whale, moon, sun, day, night, arrow, flower, salmon, and pine tree.

Cardero described how the basics of Catholicism were taught using music and rote repetition in this entry, reprinted in Donald C. Cutter's *California in 1792:*

"At the hours of prayer and instruction, the children's choir resounded as it intoned the prayers of the church; they recited the part of the catechism that they knew and repeated the words of the part they still didn't know, which the catechist kept on telling them with the greatest of patience."

He also included a trilingual version of the twenty-four sets of questions and answers that the person who was teaching, namely the catechist, repeated. The first question was stated as How many gods are there? (Answer: A single true God.) The second question was Where is God? (Answer: In Heaven, on earth, and in everything.) And so the list continued, until it reached the final entry, which was Amen.

at the missions. In a subtle way, the importance of religion in daily life was mirrored in the very size of the mission church. Of all the buildings at a mission, the church itself was always the tallest, the most massive, and the most beautifully built. When British naval Captain George Vancouver visited San Francisco in 1792, this is how he described the mission church:

> For its magnitude, architecture and internal decorations, [the church] did great credit to [its] constructors. . . . Raising and decorating this edifice appeared to have greatly attracted the attention of the fathers; the comforts they might have provided in their own hum-

A friar in Spain sculpts a model in the company of others. California missionaries longed for such companionship.

ble habitations seemed to have been totally sacrificed to the accomplishment of this favorite object. [42]

In addition, specific teachings were illustrated and reinforced in the decorations inside the church. During his 1786 visit to California, Frenchman Jean-François de Galoup de La Pérouse wrote that he believed the paintings were useful tools for neophytes' religious training. In particular, he found a painting of Hell a powerful way to frighten neophytes with what would happen to them if they did not remain good Catholics. He described the interior of the mission chapel at Carmel this way:

> The church is . . . dedicated to Saint Charles, and adorned with some tolerable pictures, copied from originals in Italy. Among them is a picture of hell . . . but as it is absolutely necessary to strike the imagination of these new converts with the most lively impressions, I am persuaded that such a representation was never more useful in any [other] country. It would be impossible for the protestant worship, which proscribes images and almost all the ceremonies of our church, to make any progress with this people. I doubt whether the picture of paradise, which sits opposite that of hell, produces so good an effect upon them. [43]

Except for the decorations on the walls and the altar, a mission church resembled a large empty hall. There were no pews or benches. The Indians stood or knelt on the floor during services. Also, the men and boys were kept on one side of the church and women and girls on the other. Someone appointed by the friar kept an aisle clear to separate the genders in an effort to keep neo-

Painting the Church

In Travis Hudson's *Breath of the Sun,* Indian Fernando Librado recalled one of the artists who decorated the interior of the Mission San Buenaventura church:

"The one who painted the pictures on the walls and ceilings of Missions San Bue-

naventura and Santa Barbara was an Indian named Juan Pacifico. Besides being a painter, he was also a singer and a musician. . . . Juan would squeeze the meat of the red tuna cactus fruit into some vessel and add the whites of eggs or pitch. He used the tail of a duck or of some kind of animal for a brush."

phytes from getting distracted. Everyone was supposed to concentrate on the lesson the friar was trying to get across.

Managing "Temporal" Affairs

In addition to their spiritual activities, friars also had many practical duties to attend to. Much was required of a successful missionary.

The friars were responsible for managing the practical business of the mission. They ran the day-to-day operations of this organization that housed and employed a thousand people or more. In the first years after a mission was founded, the friars often worked in the fields clearing land, planting seed, and harvesting crops. They had two reasons to do this work. For one, there was much work to be done. For another, they wanted to set a good example for the Indians, showing them that everyone needed to participate.

Directly or indirectly, the friars managed all economic activities at the missions—from farming and ranching to construction, building dams and irrigation ditches, weaving, candle making, and tending the sick. As the mission populations grew over the years, the friars did less hands-on work and more management. Eventually the friars became top-level managers. In this capacity the friars supervised the majordomos, *alcaldes,* and

other overseers, who in turn supervised groups of neophyte workers.

Paperwork and Bureaucracy

In addition to managing people, the friars spent a lot of time on paperwork. The Spanish Crown and the Franciscan order wanted to know what was happening at the missions in exhaustive detail. Friars spent many hours documenting their activities and the activities and progress of the converts.

At each mission the friars kept four separate registry books, one each for baptisms, confirmations, marriages, and burials. In another register, called the *Padrón,* the friars maintained an alphabetical listing of all the neophytes at the mission. The *Padrón* included each neophyte's birth date, the village where they were born, and the date of baptism. Pedro Font, a friar from Mexico who visited the mission at Carmel in 1776, describes how the missionaries used the *Padrón* to monitor the neophyte population under their control:

On Sundays and feast days the Fathers shall exercise great vigilance lest any one neglect the principal Mass or the sermon which must be preached during that holy Sacrifice. . . . When holy Mass is concluded, one of the missionaries shall call

Friars were responsible for keeping detailed records and prepared registry books containing statistics on the lives of the neophytes.

everyone by name from the Padrón. The neophytes shall then approach one after the other to kiss the priest's hand. Thus it will be seen when any one is missing.[44]

At each mission, the friars also maintained what was called the *Libro de Patentes*. This was a logbook which included handmade copies of each of the letters the mission received from any official at the College of San Fernando, as well as those from the father-president of the missions and sometimes those of the Catholic bishop in Sonora. The *Libro de Patentes* also included copies of the mission's annual reports. In an age before typewriters and photocopiers, the friars spent countless hours drawing up the reports and copying each by hand so that they had

the duplicate and triplicate copies needed to be sent to Mexico and Spain.

Reports

The friars at each mission also wrote annual reports on the state of their missions. The father-president collected all the reports from individual missions and then created a summary in duplicate. He sent one copy of the summary to the governor and one copy to the guardian of the College of San Fernando in Mexico City. These reports included some information that did not change from year to year, including the names of the missions, date of their founding, latitude, and distance from the nearest mission. They also included information that was updated with each report: the number of baptisms, marriages, and deaths from the date of the mission's founding, the number of Christians living at the mission, the number of domestic animals, the quantities of grain and vegetables sown and harvested, and the names of the missionaries serving at each of the missions. Because California's mission economy was based so heavily on farming, the annual reports included even weather reports, and other kinds of information found in an almanac.

In addition to the standard annual reports, missionaries had to write special reports when the guardian of the College of San Fernando requested them. Usually, he requested special reports after he had received accusations of wrongdoing at the missions. Because the college was in Mexico City and the guardian never visited the far-off province of California, the only way he could find out what was happening was to ask for a report. For example, in the 1790s, presidio commanders, who believed that they could run the missions better than the friars, complained that neophytes were forced to work too hard and were not properly fed. In response, the guardian sent a detailed questionnaire to the missionaries asking them to explain and justify their treatment of the

Telling Time

The friars told time using both sundials and clocks. The clocks, kept in the friars' living quarters, were particularly useful on cloudy days and as the seasons changed. In *Indian Life at the Old Missions* historian Edith Buckland Webb describes a sundial that archaeologists found in a dig at the Carmel mission:

"All around the dial, carved in stone, were objects and figures indicating, apparently, the various duties to be performed by the neophytes at the hour marked by the shadow of the gnomon [the blade that stands up from the base]. For instance, there were carved figures of kneeling Indians calling attention to the hour of prayer; figures of Indians partaking of food—an immense kettle in which it had been cooked indicating the time for breakfast, dinner, and supper. Then there were shown sheep tended by shepherds, workers in shops and fields, reminding the Indians that it was time for work when the shadow touched that spot."

Indian Fernando Librado lived at Mission San Buenaventura from childhood. His recollections appear in Travis Hudson's *Breath of the Sun*. Librado's account of telling time at the mission is included in Hudson's book.

"The priest would stand and watch his shadow and tell what time of day it was. . . . A pillar was here, made of concrete and brick, nicely finished, and on top of it was a stick. The stick had mounted on top of it a board in the shape of a half-moon. It was in width about one-half stave of a barrel. As the sun rose, it would strike [a] number. . . . This was a Christian custom.

The Indians themselves knew the time by the rising of the sun over Conejo Mountain. That mountain has many points of rock, and the Indians had a way of ascertaining the time of day accordingly. I never understood how it was calculated. . . . Diego Fernandez, an Indian, would stand about mid-day and watch his shadow: if it fell due north, he knew it was twelve o'clock."

neophytes. The friars had to answer questions on everything from what the neophytes ate and what clothing they wore to the kinds and amount of work they were required to perform, what punishments they received, and how they spent their leisure time.

Rules

The friars followed the rules for running the missions set forth by both the Franciscan order and Spanish government. Most friars welcomed the rules and structure provided because the task of running a mission was enormous. Authorities in Mexico City were too far away to give personalized advice to individual missionaries.

In 1806 the guardian of the College of San Fernando reiterated the detailed and practical rules for the California missionaries. They provided explicit instruction on many aspects of a friar's responsibilities. The rules specified common practices for record keeping, including how to account for friars' travel expenses and the need to copy all official correspondence into each mission's log book, the *Libro de Patentes*. The rules also described a mission's religious obligations to the neophytes and which religious holidays required special processions and the celebration of high mass.

The guardian's instructions mandated that bells should be used to call all neophytes to church for services every morning and every evening, and which prayers should be recited and which songs sung during regular and holiday services. They also explained what neophytes should be taught during Lent, before the annual confession, and before holy Communion. The guardian's instructions even specified a three-week waiting period between the time a couple announced

The guardian of the College of San Fernando provided detailed instructions covering the friars' responsibilities. The frequent use of mission bells was explicitly required.

their engagement and when the wedding ceremony could be performed.

In these rules the guardian also included practical measures for dealing with neophytes. Neophytes could not be required to work more than five or six hours a day in winter or six or seven hours a day in summer, except during the period when crops were sown or harvested. Physical punishments were limited to twenty-five lashes and shackles or stocks. If the crime was particularly bad, an additional six to eight lashes could be administered after a few days. Also, women were to be punished in private (in the *monjerío*) and only by another woman.

Finally the guardian reminded the friars that they must maintain their vows of poverty and chastity. In this and other matters, the guardian was repeating both general and specific guidelines that had been stated before.

The Vow of Poverty

As members of the Franciscan order, the friars had taken a vow of poverty. Georg H. von Langsdorff, a scientist with a Russian voyage to California in 1806, explained how he understood this vow: "None of the missionaries can acquire any property, so that the idea of enriching themselves can never divert their thoughts from their religious avocations. Everything they can save, or gain, goes into the chest of the establishment; they consequently return to their own country as poor as they left it."[45]

Each missionary was granted a small annual stipend or salary. The stipend was paid directly to the College of San Fernando and put on the account for the mission. It was spent in Mexico to purchase goods for the mission (including tools, food, and articles for the church) and whatever clothing or special personal items the friar might need.

Being true to their vow of poverty, friars were never supposed to handle money. However, the friars were responsible for setting prices for how much the mission would be paid for work neophytes performed at the presidios, for goods bought and sold, and for contracting the services of skilled workers and master artisans. They also kept accounting record books of all transactions, which required considerable skill in financial management.

Dressing with Humility

As Franciscans, the friars could not own anything. Their simple clothing was just one way

Contracted by a mission to provide work at a presidio, Indians spin yarn that will be fashioned into rope.

they showed their respect for the Franciscan vow of poverty. When they entered the order, they had agreed to live without personal possessions. Even their clothing and handkerchiefs belonged to the mission. Each friar had either one or two habits, which he wore every day for a year or more. When a habit could no longer be repaired, he could request a replacement.

A friar even had to make a special request to be sent a handkerchief. (Handkerchiefs were sent to California in ones and twos, never in a bundle of a dozen.) As Father Juan Crespí humbly wrote to the guardian of the College of San Fernando in Mexico City, just after arriving with the first land expedition to San Diego in 1768,

Although I have my good habit, the old one has been worn out in this long journey all the way through the mountains, and so when opportunity offers I should be glad if you would send me a habit with a hood and a tunic and cord, for here there is nothing of which to make them. I am also greatly in need of some handkerchiefs for the dust; four or six might be sent, since they are so far away—thick

Men of Power

The former neophyte Pablo Tac, who was living in Italy when he wrote *Indian Life and Customs*, likened a friar to a king. His statistics were inaccurate but the sentiment was true when he wrote:

"In the Mission of San Luis Rey de Francia the . . . [friar] is like a king. He has pages, alcaldes, majordomos, musicians, soldiers, gardens, ranchos, livestock, horses by the thousand, cows, bulls by the thousand, oxen, mules, asses, 12,000 lambs, 200 goats, etc."

Although friars dressed humbly and had few possessions, they, like European kings, controlled large properties and the actions of many people.

ones from Puebla, for I have only two, . . . and they are already badly worn, and since I have been in this country I have not been able to get any. I also ask you for a good encased crucifix for the rosary, for the one that I have is breaking. This is a favor for which I shall be very grateful, and God will reward you for it. Pardon me for troubling you. [46]

The only time a friar donned elegant clothing was to celebrate mass. At mass, friars wore lavish vestments to show dignity and their respect for the church. Sacred wear was supposed to be fancy both in respect for its sacredness and to impress the congregation of Indians.

Friars were not supposed to wear shoes or own any jewelry. When a friar died, he had nothing to leave family or friends except sometimes a pen or a handkerchief.

Among the jewelry prohibited to friars were watches. Yet the friars needed to know the time because they were responsible for having the bells rung to call the mission community to church services, to work, and to meals. Without watches that they could carry with them, friars were forced to rely on either sundials (when the sun was out) or a mantle clock inside the mission.

Friars were even forbidden to ride horses or mules by the Rule St. Francis had laid down when he founded the order in the 13th century. Friars were supposed to walk wherever they went and never ride a mule unless they were too ill to walk or the guardian himself authorized them to. Under no circumstances were they allowed to ride in a wheeled vehicle. In 1820, in a missive from the guardian of the College of San Fernando, the missionaries were warned not to ride in carts when they should walk. "To such a height has rumor mounted . . . that the missionaries of Alta California are said to go about in vehicles of two wheels and carriages of four wheels. . . . I do not doubt it will be said that the poor missionary fathers . . . enjoy themselves to an extent such that they ride in carts and carriages, a thing becoming the rich and powerful but not the poor." [47]

Home Life

Even the physical layout of the mission and the rooms assigned to the friars followed rules that applied to all missions. In the mission quadrangle, each friar had his own two-room suite: a bedroom and a sitting room, where he could welcome guests. In the bedroom, the bed was usually a dried cowhide that was stretched between four wooden posts. The blankets were those woven at the mission. They did not use sheets or pillows. The visiting French nobleman, La Pérouse, was moved to remark, "But the missionaries have hitherto been more attentive to their heavenly than their earthly concerns. . . . They are so austere as to their own comforts that they have no fireplace in their chambers, though the winter is sometimes severe." [48]

The two friars at a mission also shared a dining room and a library. Most books in the library addressed religious themes such as sermons and the lives of saints. A few of the volumes described practical matters. The friars used these to learn important skills they needed at the mission such as agriculture, architecture, and construction techniques.

Servants, chosen from among the neophytes, prepared the friars' meals. (It was routine to have servants during that time period, as getting food and preparing it was a lot harder and more time-consuming than today.) The friars ate meals apart from the neophytes and enjoyed a different diet, which

A historical representation of a friar's dining room is on display at Mission San Juan Capistrano. The friars, whose diet was based on European fare, dined apart from the neophytes.

included cheeses, wine, and other foods familiar to a European palate.

During the day many friars chewed on a kind of crushed tobacco, called snuff. After dinner they liked smoking cigars. After the midday meal they took about an hour to relax or nap (a siesta) before work began again. They had another hour or two in the evening after supper to relax and maybe read by the light of tallow candles in the library or play cards.

Travelers Brought News and Companionship

Even though the friars were surrounded by people in the missions, they felt homesick for Spain and the company of other Europeans. Time and distance cut them off from col-

leagues elsewhere. According to Georg H. von Langsdorff, a scientist accompanying the Russian voyage to California in 1806,

Posts go regularly from Vera Cruz to each of the [Spanish colonies] of North and South America. It takes a courier about two months to come from Mexico to the Presidio de San Francisco, which is the farthest establishment to the north, and European news is usually received in from five to six months after its dispatch from Madrid. Any one can with the greatest safety travel from the Presidio de San Francisco as far as Chile. Stations are located all the way, with mounted soldiers on guard.[49]

Most friars were so busy with day-to-day activities, they rarely left their mission for more than a few days every couple of years. Each mission was isolated from the others by at least one day's journey (even more in the early years of the mission period). Unless they were transferring to a new mission or returning to Mexico, the only time a friar might leave his mission was in April, when one friar from each of several nearby missions gathered to renew their vows. (One friar would stay behind at each mission to keep the mission running.)

Sometimes a year would pass between visits with other friars, the father-president, or outsiders. The arrival of a traveler was a rare and welcome event at a mission. When a newcomer was sighted, boys were sent to ring the bells, announcing the newcomer's arrival. The friars could count on a day or maybe even a week or more of shared meals and conversation.

Living so far into the frontier for many years at a time, they craved news and the fellowship of people with similar backgrounds. The French visitor Auguste Duhaut-Cilly reported of his arrival at the Santa Barbara mission in 1827. By way of introduction, he greeted an old friar he met with:

"I am French; I have come from Paris and I can give you recent news of Spain."

No [charm] ever produced a more magical effect than these few words, whose power to gain the friendly interest of these good fathers I had already experienced. . . . No sooner had I pronounced the words than the old man, starting out of his lethargy, so overwhelmed me with

gratitude and with urgent questions that I could scarcely find an instant to reply. He regained some of his lost vigor in speaking of the native land that he would never see again.[50]

A Practical Life for Spiritual Men

Every day, the friars spent many hours serving both the religious and practical needs of the mission community as a whole. Yet, far from home, the missionaries still maintained the regimentation of their order while striving toward their spiritual and missionary goals. As the German scientist Georg H. von Langsdorff said in 1806,

When one considers that in this way two or three [friars] take upon themselves such a sort of voluntary exile from their country, only to spread Christianity, and to civilize a wild and uncultivated race of men, to teach them husbandry and various useful arts, cherishing and instructing them as if they were their own children, providing them with dwellings, food, and clothing, with everything else necessary for their subsistence, and maintaining the utmost order and regularity of conduct—when all these particulars, I say, are considered, one cannot sufficiently admire the zeal and activity that carry them through labors so arduous, nor forbear to wish the most complete success to their undertaking.[51]

Daily Life of the *Gente de Razón*

A mission was largely—but not completely—a community of friars and neophytes. The other people who either lived at the missions or had frequent contact there were known as *gente de razón*. The term *gente de razón* means people of reason or intelligence and included the descendants of anyone born in Spain or Mexico, or more accurately, everyone except the indigenous California population.

Many of the *gente de razón* were soldiers and their families. Others were explorers, government representatives, skilled artisans, and other people from the Spanish colonies. Some came to California temporarily, others settled permanently.

Many Faces

Gente de razón included people of many different origins. Some were full-blooded Indians who grew up in Mexico and were Christians before they came to California.

Missions functioned as communities of friars and neophytes; however, gente de razón, *or non-indigenous Californians who were not Franciscans, also played a prominent role in mission life.*

Leather Jackets

Miguel Costansó, a soldier himself and the diarist with the first party that explored north from San Diego to Monterey, had high praise for the soldiers in the exploring party. This is how he described them in his *Discovery of San Francisco Bay:*

"They are men of great fortitude and patience in fatigue; obedient, resolute, and active, and we do not hesitate to say they are the best horsemen in the world, and among those soldiers who best earn their bread for the august monarch whom they serve.

They use a sort of leather apron, called *armas* or *defensas,* which, fastened to the pommel of the saddle, hangs down on both sides, covering their thighs and legs, that they may not hurt themselves when riding through the woods. Their offensive arms are the lance—which they handle adroitly on horseback—the broadsword, and a short musket, which they carry securely fastened in its case."

Some were descended from African slaves. Some were descended from Spaniards.

Until Mexico fought its war for independence from Spain in the 1810s, people who had been born in Spain enjoyed the highest prestige in New Spain. They had access to the best jobs and political positions. All of the friars, most top government officials, and the elite cavalry were Spaniards.

Those who were born in the New World but of full-blooded Spanish parents, were called criollos. Many military officers and government personnel were criollos, as were some of the foot soldiers. Criollos held a rank in society just below Spaniards until Mexico won its independence from Spain in 1821. After that, people born in Spain were distrusted as royalists who might still be loyal to the government that had just been toppled, and criollos gained greater status.

Many *gente de razón* were people of mixed races, with parents or grandparents descended from African slaves, native Mexican Indians, and Spaniards. A mix of African and European were called mulattos. Those of native Mexican Indian–European descent were called mestizos. Many had parents or grandparents of one race mixture who had married a person of another race mixture. Because there were many economic opportunities in California, *gente de razón* of mixed-race parents could work hard and improve their social status somewhat.

Among people of mixed-race parentage, those who could claim at least one Spanish or criollo ancestor were favored. According to Charles Henry Dana, who sailed to California from Boston in 1835, Spanish blood gave a person status and greater access in mission-period California. As he saw it:

Yet the least drop of Spanish blood, if it be only a quadroon or octoroon [one Spanish grandparent or great grandparent], is sufficient to raise one from the position of a serf and entitle him to wear a suit of clothes—boots, hat, cloak, spurs, long knife, all complete though coarse and dirty as they may be—and call himself *Español,* and to hold property if he could get any.[52]

In 1776 the total number of *gente de razón* in California was small, and most of these—about seventy—were soldiers. By 1800 the number of soldiers had risen to more than two hundred, and nonmilitary *gente de razón* numbered around five hundred.

The Sword Helps the Cross

All along, soldiers and friars shared the journey into California. The missions combined the force of the military and the power of the religious. Soldiers provided many services, both military and nonmilitary. For example, the exploring parties that ventured out in search of sites for new missions were made up mostly of soldiers. In addition, whenever a friar needed to leave a mission—to recruit new Indians, to care for the sick and dying, or to visit another mission—he needed at least one soldier to accompany him. Many of the soldiers' responsibilities were performed at the missions themselves.

The first two missions in California, San Diego and Monterey, were situated near military garrisons called presidios. Eventually two more presidios were built (at San Francisco and Santa Barbara) for a total of four presidios to protect the California's twenty-one missions.

An Escort at the Missions

About half the soldiers in California were stationed at the presidios, and the other half were stationed at missions as part of a small military force called an *escolta*, or "escort" guard. The *escolta* was made up of four to ten ordinary soldiers and one corporal, who lived at the mission. The *escolta* soldiers were under the command of the local presidio and were borrowed from presidio ranks.

When he visited San Francisco with a Russian ship in 1806, the German scientist Georg H. von Langsdorff was not impressed with the strength of the military at either the

Only a few soldiers resided at each mission. A soldier's bed and belongings, actual relics of the mission period, are pictured here at Mission San Juan Capistrano.

presidio or the nearby missions. Yet, he pointed out, the *escolta* was sufficient to maintain control at the missions.

> The number of soldiers being so small and their services so slight, it does not seem worthwhile to maintain an establishment for them. The Presidio de San Francisco has not more than forty, and it has three missions under its protection. These are San Francisco, Santa Clara, and San José. . . . There are seldom more than from three to five soldiers at any time at any mission, but this seemingly small number has hitherto been always found sufficient to keep the Indians under proper restraint.[53]

Sentinel Duty

The *escolta*'s job was to police the mission, break up fights that might occur, and watch for trouble. To do this, one of the *escolta* soldiers stood guard as a sentinel. If a sentinel saw signs of trouble he would sound the alarm to call for backup from other members of the *escolta* or from the closest presidio.

All soldiers in the *escolta* guard took turns working as sentinel at the mission. One or more sentinels were posted to guard the mission around the clock. During the day a sentinel was on duty for six hours at a time, one from 6 A.M. to noon, another from noon till 6 P.M. From 6 P.M. until morning, the shift changed every three hours.

Peace-Keeping at the Mission

Usually, the mere presence of the *escolta* guard was sufficient to keep the peace at a mission. However, sometimes soldiers were sent to capture runaway neophytes. At the missions, the soldiers punished neophytes accused of wrongdoing.

The sentinels' presence at the mission acted as a deterrent, helping to enforce order and discipline among the neophytes. Occasionally, however, disturbances broke out anyway.

The largest neophyte revolt happened in 1824. The incident was triggered when a neophyte was harshly flogged by a soldier at Mission Santa Inés. The revolt soon spread to the neighboring missions of La Purísima, Santa Barbara, and San Buenaventura. Soldiers from the Monterey presidio came to Santa Inés and bombarded the neophytes who were fortified inside the mission there. The battle lasted only a few hours but left sixteen neophytes dead and many wounded. One soldier also died.

Soldiers had carried out floggings and other punishments of neophytes from the earliest days of the mission period. What was different about this incident is that it occurred during a decade of increasing tension between soldiers and neophytes. The soldiers, who did not raise their own food, depended on supplies shipped from Mexico until about 1810, when supply ships stopped coming to California. During this period, the soldiers were angry that they had not been paid. They turned to the missions and neophytes, demanding food and other supplies but without any promise of reimbursing them.

Defense Against Nonmission Indians

Sometimes the military was called to protect the missions from nonmission Indians, especially at new missions. For example, an attack

Most of the *gente de razón* who came to California came with the hope of improving their lot in life. Some people even found that racial prejudice against them lessened after they lived in California for a while. Historian Jack D. Forbes found that the definition of a person's race often changed after a few years in California. In his article "Black Pioneers: The Spanish-Speaking Afroamericans of the Southwest," he explains:

"In general, as the status of a person improved, his race changed. He might begin life as a Negro, pure or otherwise, and end life as a *mulatto* or Eurafrican, *mestizo* or Eurindian, or even as *Español*.

An ambitious dark-skinned man might marry a light-skinned girl and produce progeny who eventually could intermarry into the 'white' upper class. . . . Such indeed is the history of the Pico family. . . . The founder of the family in California, Santiago Pico, was a mestizo, while his wife was mulatto. His sons, José Dolores, José María, Miguel, Patricio, and Francisco rose in stature by acquiring property and serving as soldiers. It was the next generation, however, which really acquired prominence; Pio Pico served as the last governor of Mexican California and Andrés Pico was a leader of the California resistance to the United States in 1846–47."

on Mission San Diego in 1776 left the buildings destroyed by fire and one friar, two soldiers, and several Indians dead.

The Tulare Indians were considered a particular threat. The Tulare lived in the hills and valleys to the east of the San Francisco Bay area. Repeatedly throughout the mission period, they attacked or stole livestock and food from the missions at Santa Clara, San José, and San Francisco. German scientist Georg H. von Langsdorff reported the stories he heard when he visited in 1806:

When Mission San José was first founded [non-Christian Indians] became troublesome from time to time. Only a year and a half before I was there they had murdered five soldiers and dangerously wounded one of the padres and another soldier. Upon this a strong military expedition was sent out against them, and a great slaughter of the Indians was the result, whereupon they were compelled to conclude a

peace. There has been no trouble with them since.[54]

Not Well Armed

Native Californian attacks were remarkably few, given that many saw the friars and other Spanish as invaders, and that the native population probably outnumbered the Spanish by one thousand to one. The Spanish military in California was able to maintain control with few real battles for several reasons: Spanish weapons were superior to those of the Indians; cannons and muskets could win a battle against arrows and spears; and the Spanish shields and vests protected them even further against Indian weapons. The Spanish cavalry's horses provided both psychological and practical advantages of speed, size, and imposing stature. In addition, the Indians had no experience in warfare beyond quick skirmishes with rival tribelets.

Soldiers carried muskets, broadswords, and lances. Their shields were made of bull hide. For armor, they wore leather vests made of seven layers of deer- or sheepskin, quilted together. Named for these vests, they were called *soldados de cuera*, or leather-jacket soldiers. The leather-jacket soldiers were highly skilled both as fighting men and as horsemen.

Protecting Against Foreign Invaders

Soldiers in California were more occupied in internal affairs at the missions and presidios than in protecting against foreign invaders. During the entire mission period, fewer than twenty foreign ships visited California. Most followed strict diplomatic protocol, asking permission to land, exchanging formal greetings with the local military command, gov-

ernment official, or friars. They collected information on the Spanish military strength there in order to inform their governments but did not pose a specific threat to the missions or presidios.

Only once were the missions directly threatened by foreign intruders. In 1818 two ships of Chileans and other Latin Americans under the command of the French pirate Hippolyte de Bouchard sailed along the California coast, and burned and looted the presidio at Monterey and Mission San Juan Capistrano. Rather than a head-on military engagement, most of the mission communities packed their bags and fled to safe locations inland for several weeks.

Presidios

California's presidios were built with defense —not offense—in mind. By today's standards,

Spanish soldiers and Indians are pictured near the presidio designed to defend the entrance to San Francisco Bay.

In addition to their role as protectors, soldiers were also talented craftsmen who performed a variety of non-military duties, such as constructing walls like the one pictured here.

they were not well armed. At first, each presidio was surrounded by a stockade of wooden poles, but soon this was replaced by more permanent mounded earth or adobe brick walls. Batteries of guns and cannons were set in the walls.

When Englishman George Vancouver visited California in 1793, he was searching for potential flaws in the defenses of rival Spain. Expecting a major military force to protect the northernmost frontier, he was surprised at the meager defenses in San Francisco:

> This sketch will be sufficient . . . to convey some idea of the inactive spirit of the people and the unprotected state of the establishment at this port, which I should conceive ought to be a principal object of the Spanish crown, as a key and barrier to their more southern and valuable settlements on the borders of the north Pacific. [The presidio] possesses no other means for its protection than . . . a brass three-pounder [cannon] on a rotten carriage before that presidio, and a similar

piece of ordnance [weaponry] which (I was told) was at the SE point of entrance lashed to a log instead of a carriage; and was the gun whose report we heard the evening of our arrival. Before the presidio there had formerly been two pieces of ordnance, but one of them had lately burst to pieces.[55]

Nonmilitary Duties

Given that strictly military duties did not consume much of the soldiers' time, most soldiers also worked at other jobs too. Spanish eyewitness José Cardero reported what he saw at the mission in Carmel in 1792:

> The lack of colonists of any other kind has obliged these soldiers to employ themselves in all of the occupations necessary for a civilized population. As a result, one can be seen acting as a sentinel of the guard; another building a wall, making a door, or sewing shoes; yet another arming himself to go into the inte-

rior along the roads to carry information to other presidios or missions.[56]

Some soldiers were primarily craftsmen, and only secondarily military men. Among the skilled craftsmen at the presidios were carpenters, blacksmiths, masons, armorers, tailors, millwrights, and master mechanics who kept all the machines in order. These people helped build and maintain the presidios and kept the army's horses shod and properly tended.

Helping the Friars

Running a mission took more hours than there were in a day and more skills than the friars had by themselves. The friars delegated many tasks to soldiers and other *gente de razón* because they could not run the missions alone. As Father Junípero Serra wrote to the Viceroy in 1773: "[A friar] cannot attend personally to everything, nor would he know how to direct all the manual work that comes up, for at the monastery they did not teach him this."[57]

Frequently the corporal of the *escolta,* or one or more of the ordinary soldiers, helped manage day-to-day activities at the mission. A person who worked as a manager at a mission was called a majordomo, or overseer. He directed the neophytes in their daily work and reported back to the friars.

Other Jobs at the Missions

Other soldiers helped keep information flowing between missions and between missions and presidios. The soldiers who served as mail carriers and couriers traveled up and down the Pacific coast. The first two missions (San Diego and Monterey) were separated by

some 450 miles, yet they needed to communicate with each other on a regular basis. As more and more missions were built the distances became shorter, but in an age before the telephone or even the telegraph, if news was to travel, someone had to take it. As often as every week or two, a packet of mail (including dispatches for government officials and correspondence for the missionaries) arrived in San Diego by land or ship from Mexico. Then, soldier-couriers rode on horseback to each of the missions and presidios, delivering what they carried and receiving outgoing correspondence and small packages.

Not all assistance was quite so mundane. For example, in 1820 the missionaries at Santa Barbara wanted special help in creating a spectacular ceremony to dedicate the newly rebuilt mission church. Father Ripoll sent the following message to Governor Pablo Vicente de Solá requesting a rocket maker to help prepare for festivities for new church dedication ceremonies:

> My dear friend and esteemed Sir: Herewith I entreat Your Honor to be pleased to send me the permit allowing a certain Salvador Béjar, a rocket-maker, to come here for two months. Being of the military company of San Diego, he may not come without license from Your Honor. We need him in order that he may prepare some fireworks for our celebration, which we have postponed to September 8. Meanwhile, Your Honor will have time to despatch your orders and also to [be present] at the feast and be the Godfather.[58]

A Soldier's Wages

Technically, the government paid soldiers' salaries. Whether they were posted to a presidio

Because Santa Barbara (pictured) and the other missions were located miles apart, a soldier-courier system was established to deliver mail regularly.

or part of a mission's *escolta* guard, a soldier's pay was calculated in money (pesos). However, because there was never much for sale in California, much of their payment was in food, supplies, and services from the missions.

Historian Maynard Geiger found several job contracts in the Santa Barbara mission archives. The contracts offered cash for providing such services as tanning hides, teaching carpentry, and teaching shoe making.

In one 1820 contract offering employment to a husband and wife team. Señor Francisco Garcia was to perform services as a locksmith and his wife, Doña María Luisa, was hired to work in the infirmary. Together, their annual salary was two hundred pesos plus the services of a servant. In addition, each week they earned two bushels of corn and one half-bushel of beans. Every month they were entitled to one quarter of a steer and some soap.

Historian Robert Archibald found the following contract, dated April 1811, for mas-

ter artisan José Antonio Ramírez to work at Mission Purísima. Included in his salary was a monthly ration of chocolate. "He binds himself to assist in making the stone basins, canals, and all washing places and drinking troughs after finishing the fountain and besides to direct the carpenter work. He will be paid 200 pesos in silver, with board, three drinks per day and two pounds of chocolate monthly."[59]

A Life Apart

Unlike the friars, the soldiers could marry and have children. Married soldiers were encouraged to bring their wives and children with them from Mexico but sometimes fiancées and even wives refused to travel so far from civilization. Many of the soldiers who were single when they arrived at the missions met and later married neophyte women who were native to California.

Both friars and government officials worried that single men serving as soldiers in California, as well as married soldiers without their families, might create problems. Lonely or bored soldiers spent their free time drinking and chasing after Indian women. Accordingly, government policies encouraged married soldiers to bring their families with them into California.

At the mission, *escolta* soldiers lived with their families in a guardhouse just outside the mission quadrangle. It was situated so that they could watch the church, the friars' quarters, and the neophytes' quarters, guarding against any possible trouble. The guardhouse was divided into separate apartments for each family. It usually had its own fruit and vegetable garden, water fountain, laundry facilities, and kitchen. The ovens were in the yard outside the guardhouse.

Soldiers' wives were active members of the mission community. They were responsible for cooking, cleaning, and other tasks to support their husbands and children as well as the bachelor soldiers in the *escolta*. They prepared meals and ate separately from the mission population. In addition, some wives worked at other jobs at the mission, including teaching young neophyte girls everything from spinning and weaving to Christianity.

Soldiers and their families were the *gente de razón* with whom the friars and neophytes had the most contact. The friars wanted them to provide a good example for the neophytes of how a Christian lived and worked. Soldiers were expected to attend church regularly, sometimes for morning mass every day, or at least for Sunday mass.

Pueblos

As time went on, the friars and neophytes from the missions also had frequent dealings with *gente de razón* in Spanish towns called pueblos. The Spanish government had first planned only missions and presidios in California but later authorized the founding of

The Spanish government worried that single soldiers would engage in drinking and would pursue Indian women. Thus, soldiers like this one were urged to bring their families with them to California.

pueblos. The pueblos were designed to increase the Hispanic population in California. They were set up as farming communities that could provide the meat, grains, vegetables, and other ingredients needed to prepare meals for the soldiers. (Until then, the presidios had purchased their supplies either from the missions or from supply ships sent up from Mexico.)

The first two pueblos were San José and Los Angeles. In 1777 the governor of California drew fourteen soldiers and their families from the presidios of San Francisco and Monterey to found San José de Guadalupe (later San José). Four years later another twelve families (forty-six persons altogether) traveled overland from northern Mexico to settle El Pueblo de Nuestra Señora la Reina de los Angeles del Río Porciúncula (later shortened to Los Angeles).

In 1797 a third pueblo, called Branciforte, was created near Mission Santa Cruz. The Spanish government wanted a stronger military in the area but could not afford to send more soldiers. Instead, they promised free land and temporary support to former soldiers who moved there. The government hoped that these settlers would become self-sufficient and thus be less expensive to maintain than presidio soldiers. Meanwhile, the settlers could act as military reservists and become active soldiers again if there was an outside military threat.

Soldiers as Settlers

One reason that soldiers were sent to the pueblos is that it was hard to attract volunteers. The mission period was almost over before California became a place where many settlers wanted to go. The territory was too isolated, and settlers had to work too hard, to

survive there. Because the missions alone did not make California a strong part of the empire, the Spanish government tried a variety of experiments to entice its citizens to move there.

At first, to encourage settlement, the government paid annual stipends in food, clothing, and supplies to those families who settled in a pueblo. Some of the settlers were convicted criminals who chose exile in California over jail time in Mexico. Soldiers who had served their tour of duty were sometimes paid to retire in a California pueblo.

The friars generally disapproved of the pueblos. Pueblos and missions competed for land, but worse, pueblo residents gave a bad example of Christian behavior. For example, in 1820 a friar at Santa Barbara, Francisco Suñer, wrote a letter to the governor saying, "Every day we see men drunk, as well from among those who call themselves [*gente de razón*], as also from among the Indians . . . , because in this presidial town and the immediate vicinity there are six or seven taverns where brandy is sold, or to speak more accurately, where every one who has a mind to, sells it in spite of the orders which Your Honor has issued."[60]

Another major complaint that the friars had was that both pueblo and presidio residents were lazy. Because of their laziness, they required mission neophytes to perform many tasks for them, from the simplest to the most highly skilled. In his annual report for 1813, Santa Barbara friar Ramón Olbés argued that everyone in a civilized community should work. He complained that the local *gente de razón* wanted to treat neophytes as slaves, not as fellow Christians:

The people in this province, known as the *gente de razón,* . . . are so lazy and indolent that they know nothing more

When George Vancouver visited the Santa Clara mission in 1792, he watched as soldiers from Santa Cruz rounded up cattle to be slaughtered for a feast. According to Vancouver, as reprinted in Joshua Paddison, *A World Transformed:*

"The [cattle] propagate very fast, and . . . live in large herds on the fertile plains of Santa Clara—in a sort of wild state. . . . Señor Paries, an ensign in the Spanish Army, . . . conceived the business of taking the cattle would be better performed by the soldiers, who are occasionally cavalry and are undoubtedly very good horsemen. We mounted and accompanied them to the field to be spectators of their exploits. Each of the soldiers was provided with a strong line made of horsehair or of thongs of leather, or rather hide, with a long running noose. This is thrown with great dexterity whilst at full speed, and nearly with a certainty, over the horns of the animals by two men, one on each side of the ox, at the same instant of time; and having a strong high peaked pummel to their saddles, each takes a turn round it with the end of the line, and by that means the animal is kept completely at bay and effectively prevented from doing either the men or the horses any injury, which they would be very liable to, from the wildness and ferocity of the cattle. In this situation the beast is led to the place of slaughter, where a third person, with equal dexterity, whilst the animal is kicking and plunging between the horses, entangles its hind legs by a rope and throws it down, on which its throat is immediately cut. . . . Twenty-two bullocks, each weighing from four to six hundred weight, were killed on this occasion."

than how to ride horseback. Labor of any kind they regard as dishonorable. They are of the opinion that only the Indians ought to work; wherefore they solicit the service of the Indians for even the most necessary things for their maintenance such as cooking, washing, doing garden work, taking care of the babies, etc.[61]

Friars Serve the Presidios and Pueblos

Gente de razón who lived at the presidios or in pueblos relied on the mission friars for all church services because there were no other priests in California for many years. The friars often celebrated mass at presidio chapels.

Nonmission *gente de razón* came to mission churches to be married and to baptize their children.

In some places, such as the pueblo of San José, the Spanish population paraded over to the nearest mission with much pomp and ceremony every Sunday. In Santa Barbara, one long-time resident described her recollections of going to the mission church for mass on Sundays:

We used to go to church attended by our (Indian) servants, who carried small mats for us to kneel upon, as there were no seats. A tasteful little rug was considered an indispensable part of our belongings, and every young lady embroidered her own. The church floors were cold, hard, and damp, and even the poorer classes

Daily Life of the *Gente de Razón* **91**

managed to use mats of some kind, usually of tule woven by the Indians.[62]

When someone was too ill to travel to the mission, a friar sometimes traveled to that person's home to provide solace or, in extreme cases, to perform last rites. When *gente de razón* died in California, they were often buried in mission cemeteries.

A Growing Community

When the first missions were founded at San Diego and Monterey, they were isolated islands of Hispanic culture. As time went on the number of missions grew, and so did the numbers of *gente de razón* who either lived at or interacted with the friars and neophytes at the missions.

Last Days of the Missions

The California missions were designed to be temporary institutions that would turn natives into Spanish citizens. Once the neophytes knew the ways of the European world (voting, paying taxes, regular work habits, Spanish language), the missions were supposed to dissolve and the neophytes become Spanish citizens.

Yet, throughout the sixty-nine years of the mission period, the Franciscan friars never believed that the neophytes were ready to move beyond the missions. Had it not been for outside economic and political forces, the missionaries might have continued to run the missions indefinitely.

By the 1830s mission prosperity had diminished. The number of neophytes at the missions was dropping. Many neophytes had died, and fewer were joining the missions. Meanwhile, more settlers had come north to California from central Mexico. The newcomers envied the vast tracts of rich, productive land

A lone clay cross, an emblem of the end of the mission era, marks the gravesite of Indians at the San Diego mission.

that the missions owned. The settlers also resented the free labor that neophytes provided at the missions.

In addition, after a ten-year war, Mexico had won its independence from Spain in 1821. At first Mexico's northern boundary was the same as the viceroyalty of New Spain's had been. That is, the country of Mexico included the territories that would later belong to the United States and become the states of Texas, New Mexico, Arizona, and California.

The new Mexican government represented both new ideals and different practical concerns. All natives of Spain—including nearly all of the Franciscan missionaries—were distrusted because of possible loyalties to the old Spanish government. Also, the new government sought to decrease the power of the Roman Catholic church and increase the rights of individuals.

Thus, in 1833 the Mexican government passed a law to turn mission communities into nonreligious towns, that is to secularize them. This put an end to the mission period.

With secularization, the church continued to own the mission chapels but the friars were to be replaced by nonmissionary priests. The friars, all Spanish-born until this time, were supposed to be expelled from California unless they signed an oath of loyalty to the new government. However, some friars refused to sign, believing this to be a traitorous act. A few friars fled the territory (usually on board American or other foreign ships) rather than sign the oath.

At this time the missions—worked by neophytes under the control of the friars—provided nearly all the food and other supplies that supported both presidio soldiers and other nonmission people. In 1825 the

Physical Decay

Edwin Bryant, born in Massachusetts in 1805, traveled by wagon train to California. Published in Joshua Paddison's *A World Transformed* is Bryant's description of what remained of Mission San José in 1846:

"Passing the squares of one-story adobe buildings, once inhabited by thousands of busy Indians, but now deserted, roofless, and crumbling into ruins, we reached the plaza in front of the church and the massive two-story edifices occupied by the padres during the flourishing epoch of the establishment. These were in good repair, but the doors and windows with the exception of one were closed, and nothing of moving life was visible except a donkey or two, standing near a fountain that gushed its waters into a capacious stone trough. . . . We entered the open door, and here we

found two Frenchmen dressed in sailor costume, with a quantity of coarse shirts, pantaloons, stockings, and other small articles, together with aguardiente, which they designed retailing to such of the natives in the vicinity as chose to become their customers. They were itinerant merchants—or peddlers—and had opened their wares here for a day or two only, or so long as they could find purchasers.

I passed through extensive warehouses and immense rooms, once occupied for the manufacture of woolen blankets and other articles, with the rude machinery still standing in them, but unemployed. Filth and desolation have taken the place of cleanliness and busy life. . . . I requested permission to examine the interior of the church but it was locked up, and no person in the mission was in possession of the key."

new Mexican governor of California, José María Echeandia, found a way to maintain the economy, at least for a while. He put the Carmel mission friar, Vicente Francisco Sarría, under house arrest but kept him in his old post at the mission. Governor Echeandia's letter to authorities in Mexico City stated:

> The departure of the [friar] and of the many Religious who would follow him, in my judgement would occasion much disquietude in the territory. . . . The lack of missionaries would cause disorder in the establishments of the neophytes who are in charge and which they have been able to preserve in the same state. I have, therefore, not urged the quick departure of Fr. Sarría until the time when a sufficient number of missionaries might relieve who by reason of the law must leave the Republic [of Mexico].[63]

Most friars, especially those who were old or ailing, stayed at the missions that had become their homes. A few new priests came but never enough to serve all of the former mission chapels or the growing population of California.

Secularization also meant that the mission lands and other mission property were to be divided between the new settlers and the neophytes. Neophytes were supposed to be granted part of all the lands that had belonged to their ancestors. All of a mission's buildings and all the livestock (cattle, sheep, goats, mules, and horses) were to be divided among the individual neophytes who lived at that mission. In fact, few neophytes received their share of mission property, and most of those who did soon lost or sold it to the new settlers.

At the end of the mission era many of the neophytes knew no other life. They had lived and worked at the missions all their lives. When they were turned away from the missions, they could not return to their ancestral villages because nearly all the Indian villages in the mission region had disappeared. Without land of their own or the knowledge needed to farm without the guidance of the friars, many neophytes became laborers on the ranches and farms of the new settlers.

Notes

Introduction: Spain in the Americas

1. Quoted in Zephyrin Engelhardt, *The Missions and Missionaries of California.* San Francisco: James H. Barry, 1912, vol. 2, p. 5.
2. Quoted in Joshua Paddison, ed., *A World Transformed: Firsthand Accounts of California Before the Gold Rush.* Berkeley, CA: Heyday, 1999, p. 181.

Chapter 1: Founding the Missions

3. Francisco Palóu, *Historical Memoirs of New California*, ed. Herbert Eugene Bolton. Berkeley: University of California Press, 1926, vol. 1, pp. 122–24.
4. Quoted in Herbert Eugene Bolton, *Fray Juan Crespí, Missionary Explorer on the Pacific Coast 1769–1774.* Berke-ley: University of California Press, 1927, p. 18.
5. Palóu, *Historical Memoirs,* vol. 2, p. 311.
6. Palóu, *Historical Memoirs,* vol. 1, pp. 51–52, vol. 2, pp. 37–38.
7. Palóu, *Historical Memoirs,* vol. 2, p. 73.
8. Quoted in Don DeNevi and Noel Francis Moholy, *Junípero Serra: The Illustrated Story of the Franciscan Founder of California's Missions.* San Francisco and New York: Harper & Row, 1985, p. 101.
9. Quoted in Zephyrin Engelhardt, *Santa Barbara Mission.* San Francisco: James H. Barry, 1923, p. 50.
10. Quoted in Engelhardt, *Santa Barbara,* pp. 104–5.

Chapter 2: The Making of a Missionary

11. Quoted in Walton Bean and James J.

Rawls, *California: An Interpretive History.* New York: McGraw-Hill, 1983, p. 36.
12. Francisco Palóu, *Life and Apostolic Labors of the Venerable Father Junípero Serra,* trans. C. Scott Williams. Pasadena, CA: G. W. James, 1913, pp. 1–2.
13. Quoted in Engelhardt, *Santa Barbara,* p. 175.
14. Quoted in DeNevi and Moholy, *Junípero Serra,* pp. 103–4.
15. Palóu, *Life of Serra,* pp. 8–9.
16. Palóu, *Life of Serra,* p. 12.
17. Quoted in Engelhardt, *Santa Barbara,* p. 152.
18. Quoted in Robert Archibald, *The Economic Aspects of the California Missions.* Washington, DC: Academy of American Franciscan History, 1978, p. 3.
19. Quoted in DeNevi and Moholy, *Junípero Serra,* p. 104.
20. Maynard Geiger, *Franciscan Missionaries in Hispanic California 1769–1848.* San Marino, CA: Huntington Library, 1969, p. xi.

Chapter 3: Recruiting Converts

21. Miguel Costansó, *The Discovery of San Francisco Bay: The Portolá Expedition of 1769–1770,* ed. Peter Browning. Lafayette, CA: Great West, 1992, p. 43.
22. Costansó, *Discovery,* p. 93.
23. Quoted in Donald C. Cutter, *California in 1792: A Spanish Naval Visit.* Norman: University of Oklahoma Press, 1990, p. 132.
24. Quoted in Paddison, *A World Transformed,* p. 33.

25. Quoted in Edith Buckland Webb, *Indian Life at the Old Missions.* Los Angeles: Warren F. Lewis, 1952, pp. 25–26.
26. Palóu, *Historical Memoirs,* vol. 1, pp. 53–57.
27. Quoted in Engelhardt, *Missions and Missionaries,* vol. 2, p. 593.
28. Quoted in "The Barrel Organ at Mission San Juan Bautista." www.standing stones.com.
29. Jean François de La Pérouse, *Monterey in 1786: Life in a California Mission.* Berkeley, CA: Heyday, 1989, p. 82.

Chapter 4: Daily Life of the Mission Indians

30. La Pérouse, *Monterey in 1786,* pp. 85–88.
31. Quoted in Cutter, *California in 1792,* p. 139.
32. Quoted in Engelhardt, *Santa Barbara,* p. 64.
33. Georg H. von Langsdorff, *Narrative of the Rezanov Voyage to Nueva California in 1806.* San Francisco: Private Press of Thomas C. Russell, 1927, pp. 64–65.
34. Auguste Duhaut-Cilly, *A Voyage to California, the Sandwich Islands, & Around the World in the Years 1826–1829,* Translated and edited by August Frugé and Neal Harlow, Berkeley: University of California Press, 1999, p. 81.
35. La Pérouse, *Monterey in 1786,* pp. 85–88.
36. Quoted in Engelhardt, *Missions and Missionaries,* vol. 2, pp. 560–61.
37. Duhaut-Cilly, *Voyage,* pp. 111, 115–16.
38. Quoted in Engelhardt, *Santa Barbara,* p. 94.
39. Quoted in Engelhardt, *Santa Barbara,* pp. 80–81.

Chapter 5: Daily Life of the Friars

40. Quoted in Engelhardt, *Missions and Missionaries,* vol. 2, p. 117.
41. Quoted in Paddison, *A World Transformed*, pp. 190–91.
42. Quoted in Paddison, *A World Transformed,* p. 82.
43. La Pérouse, *Monterey in 1786,* p. 78.
44. Quoted in Engelhardt, *Missions and Missionaries,* vol. 2, p. 255.
45. Quoted in Engelhardt, *Missions and Missionaries,* vol. 2, p. 636.
46. Bolton, *Fray Juan Crespi,* pp. 19–20.
47. Quoted in Irving Berdine Richman, *California under Spain and Mexico 1535–1847.* Boston and New York: Houghton Mifflin, 1911, p. 466.
48. La Pérouse, *Monterey in 1786,* p. 87.
49. von Langsdorff, *Narrative,* pp. 122–23.
50. Duhaut-Cilly, *Voyage,* p. 79.
51. Quoted in Paddison, *A World Transformed,* p. 109.

Chapter 6: Daily Life of the *Gente de Razón*

52. Quoted in Sydney Temple, *The Carmel Mission.* Santa Cruz, CA: Western Tanager, 1980, pp. 81–82.
53. Quoted in Paddison, *A World Transformed*, p. 107.
54. Langsdorff, *Narrative,* pp. 107–8.
55. Quoted in Paddison, *A World Transformed,* pp. 76–77.
56. Quoted in Cutter, *California in 1792,* p. 121.
57. Quoted in Archibald, *Economic Aspects,* p. 78.
58. Quoted in Engelhardt, *Santa Barbara,* p. 107.

59. Quoted in Archibald, *Economic Aspects*, p. 152.

60. Quoted in Engelhardt, *Santa Barbara*, p. 147.

61. Quoted in Engelhardt, *Santa Barbara*, p. 98.

62. Quoted in Engelhardt, *Santa Barbara*, p. 114.

Epilogue: Last Days of the Missions

63. Quoted in Temple, *Carmel Mission*, pp. 75–76.

For Further Reading

Emily Abbink, *Missions of the Monterey Bay Area.* Minneapolis, MN: Lerner, 1996. Describes the missions of Carmel, Santa Cruz, and San Juan Bautista, and life among the Ohlone Indians before the arrival of the Spaniards.

June Behrens, *Missions of the Central Coast.* Minneapolis, MN: Lerner, 1996. Describes the California missions of Santa Barbara, La Purísima Concepción, and Santa Inés, and life among the Chumash Indians before the arrival of the Spaniards.

Pauline Brower, *Missions of the Inland Valleys.* Minneapolis, MN: Lerner, 1996. Describes the missions of San Antonio, San Luís Obispo, Nuestra Senora de la Soledad, and San Miguel, and life of the inland valley Indian tribes, many of whom were Salinan, before the arrival of the Spaniards.

Nancy Lemke, *Missions of the Southern Coast.* Minneapolis, MN: Lerner, 1996. Describes the California missions of San Diego, San Juan Capistrano, and San Luis Rey, and life among the Indians of southwestern California before the arrival of the Spaniards.

Dianne MacMillan, *Missions of the Los Angeles Area.* Minneapolis, MN: Lerner, 1996. Describes the missions of San Gabriel Arcángel, San Buenaventura, and San Fernando, and life among the Tongva (Gabrielino) and Chumash Indians before the arrival of the Spaniards.

Elizabeth Van Steenwyk, *The California Missions.* New York: Franklin Watts, 1995. An easy overview of life in all the missions.

Tekla N. White, *Missions of the San Francisco Bay Area.* Minneapolis, MN: Lerner, 1996. Describes the missions of San Francisco, Santa Clara, San José, San Rafael, and San Francisco Solano (Sonoma), and life among the Ohlone and Coast Miwok Indians before the arrival of the Spaniards.

Works Consulted

Books

Robert Archibald, *The Economic Aspects of the California Missions.* Washington, DC: Academy of American Franciscan History, 1978. A thorough scholarly work.

Hubert Howe Bancroft, *California Pastoral: 1769–1848.* San Francisco: History Company, 1888. Like *History of California,* a rich source of information.

———, *History of California.* Vol. 1. San Francisco: A.L. Bancroft & Company, 1884. One of the standard works that other scholars draw upon. Based on the many interviews and printed materials relating to California history that Bancroft collected.

Walton Bean and James J. Rawls, *California: An Interpretive History.* New York: McGraw-Hill, 1983. A good introduction.

Herbert Eugene Bolton, *Fray Juan Crespí, Missionary Explorer on the Pacific Coast 1769–1774.* Berkeley: University of California Press, 1927. A great primary source, this chronicles what Crespí saw and heard when he traveled with the explorers and founding parties of several early missions.

John Bowker, ed., *The Oxford Dictionary of World Religions.* Oxford and New York: Oxford University Press, 1997. Provides solid definitions and explanations of religious concepts.

Sherburne Friend Cook, *The Conflict Between the California Indian and White Civilization.* Berkeley and Los Angeles: University of California Press, 1943. An important work on the clash of cultures. Emphasis on the period after secularization.

Miguel Costansó, *The Discovery of San Francisco Bay: The Portolá Expedition of 1769–1770.* Ed. Peter Browning. Lafayette, CA: Great West, 1992. The diary of one of the members of the first exploring party that traveled from San Diego to San Francisco and Monterey. Printed in English and Spanish.

Donald C. Cutter, *California in 1792: A Spanish Naval Visit.* Norman: University of Oklahoma Press, 1990. Includes the journal of José Cardero, who traveled with the Spanish schooners *Sutil* and *Mexicana.*

Don DeNevi and Noel Francis Moholy, *Junípero Serra: The Illustrated Story of the Franciscan Founder of California's Missions.* San Francisco and New York: Harper & Row, 1985. Provides lots of detail and praise about Serra.

Auguste Duhaut-Cilly, *A Voyage to California, the Sandwich Islands, & Around the World in the Years 1826–1829.* Translated and edited by August Frugé and Neal Harlow. Berkeley: University of California Press, 1999. A colorful picture.

Alice Eastwood, ed., "Archibald Menzies' Journal of the Vancouver Expedition," *California Historical Society Quarterly.* Vol. 2, no. 4, January 1924.

Zephyrin Engelhardt, *The Missions and Missionaries of California.* Vol. 2. San Francisco: James H. Barry, 1912. Based on materials in the Santa Barbara Mission archive, these volumes by a Franciscan scholar provide the basis for many other scholars.

————, *Santa Barbara Mission*. San Francisco: James H. Barry, 1923. Based on primary source materials in the Santa Barbara Mission archive.

Jack D. Forbes, "Black Pioneers: The Spanish-Speaking Afroamericans of the Southwest," in George E. Frakes and Curtis B. Solberg, eds., *Minorities in California History*. New York: Random House, 1971. An excellent view of the topic.

Maynard Geiger, *Franciscan Missionaries in Hispanic California 1769–1848*. San Marino, CA: Huntington Library, 1969. Well-researched biographies of all the Franciscan missionaries.

————, *Mission Santa Barbara 1782–1965*. Santa Barbara,CA: Franciscan Fathers of California, 1965. Draws on rich primary sources in Santa Barbara.

Charles Gibson, ed., *The Spanish Tradition in America*. New York: Harper & Row, 1968. A compilation of official documents.

Travis Hudson, ed., *Breath of the Sun: Life in Early California As Told by a Chumash Indian, Fernando Librado to John P. Harrington*. Banning, CA: Malki Museum, 1979. Fernando Librado was around one hundred years old when anthropologist John Harrington first interviewed him in 1912. Here, based on interview transcripts, Librado recalls his life both during the last years of the mission period and later.

George Wharton James, *In and Out of the Old Missions of California*. Boston: Little, Brown and Company, 1905. Written in a period of revival of interest in the missions, this quotes and draws on a variety of sources to provide a view into daily life at the missions.

Dorothy Krell, et al. eds., *The California Missions, A Pictorial History*. Menlo Park, CA: Sunset Books, 1979. An excellent and visually pleasing look at each of the California missions, both during the mission period and through more recent calamities and reconstructions.

Alfred Louis Kroeber, *Handbook of the Indians of California*. Berkeley: California Book Company, 1953. The standard work on native California.

Georg H. von Langsdorff, *Narrative of the Rezanov Voyage to Nueva California in 1806*. Trans. Thomas C. Russell. San Francisco: Private Press of Thomas C. Russell, 1927. An important view of the area around San Francisco, written by a doctor and scientist employed on a Russian ship. Parts of the journal have been printed in other sources.

Jean-François de Galoup de La Pérouse, *Monterey in 1786: Life in a California Mission*. Berkeley, CA: Heyday, 1989. The journal of this French nobleman while he was visiting in Monterey.

Joshua Paddison, ed., *A World Transformed: Firsthand Accounts of California Before the Gold Rush*. Berkeley, CA: Heyday, 1999. A good compendium of primary source materials.

Francisco Palóu, *Historical Memoirs of New California*. Vols. 1 and 2. Ed. Herbert Eugene Bolton, Berkeley: University of California Press, 1926. The best contemporary account of the early mission period.

——, *Life and Apostolic Labors of the Venerable Father Junípero Serra*. Trans. C. Scott Williams. Pasadena, CA: G. W. James, 1913. A biography of Junípero Serra by his friend and colleague.

Irving Berdine Richman, *California under Spain and Mexico 1535–1847*. Boston and New York: Houghton Mifflin, 1911. Dated but still a rich source, with emphasis on government, military, and religious leaders.

Andrew F. Rolle, *California: A History*. 5th ed. Wheeling, IL: Harlan Davidson, 1998. A basic overview from ancient times to the present.

Pablo Tac, *Indian Life and Customs at Mission San Luis Rey: A Record of California Mission Life*. Trans. Minna Hewes and Gordon Hewes. San Luis Rey, CA: Old Mission, 1958. Written in Italy when Tac was about thirteen, this is the only account of Indian life written by an Indian during the mission period.

Sydney Temple, *The Carmel Mission*. Santa Cruz, CA: Western Tanager, 1980. A good overview of the history of this mission.

Edith Buckland Webb, *Indian Life at the Old Missions*. Los Angeles: Warren F. Lewis, 1952. A rich look into life at the missions.

Websites

The Barrel Organ at Mission San Juan Bautista (www.standingstones.com). A compilation of quotes and commentary on various aspects of music at Mission San Juan Bautista.

California Mission Studies Association (www.ca-missions.org). An excellent reference tool that includes a glossary, a bibliography, and information about the association.

The Catholic Encyclopedia (www.newadvent.org). Comprehensive source of information on both current and historical people and terminology related to the Roman Catholic Church.

Index

adobe (clay brick), 24, 55–57, 59
agriculture. *See* farming
alcalde (mission Indian leader), 52, 68
Alexander VI (pope), 12
  see also pope, the
Alta California, 10
  see also California
Apostolic College of San Fernando.
  See College of San Fernando

Baja California, 10
baptism, 46–47
Beechey, Frederick William, 11, 42,
  68–69
"Black Pioneers: The Spanish-Speaking
  Afroamericans of the Southwest"
  (Forbes), 84
Bolton, Herbert Eugene, 35
Bouchard, Hippolyte de, 85
Branciforte, 90
Breath of the Sun: Life in Early California
  (Hudson), 56, 59, 71, 73
Bryant, Edwin, 94
Bucareli, Antonio Mariá de, 67

Cabrillo, Juan Rodríguez, 37
California, 10, 11–13, 35
  see also Indians
California in 1792: A Spanish Naval Visit
  (Cutter), 32, 47, 51, 61, 64
Cardero, José, 32
  baptism of Indians and, 47
  clothing of mission population and, 61
  Indians and, 40–41
  mission religious education and, 69
  sharing of property and, 52

  soldiers' work and, 87
Carmel (mission)
  clothing at, 61
  decoration of, 70
  dictionary of Indian language at, 69
  education of Indians at, 69
  food and meals at, 51
  military and, 82
  site of, 17–18
  sundial at, 73
Carrillo, Raymundo, 20
Catholicism, 10–12, 25, 26
cattle. *See* cowboys; ranching
Clare of Assisi, Saint, 28
clocks, 73
clothing, 61
College of San Fernando, 22, 32–34,
  72–74
  see also Franciscan missionaries;
    Mexico City
construction, 55–57
Costansó, Miguel, 16, 37–38, 81
cowboys, 54–55, 91
  see also ranching
Crespí, Juan, 16, 18–19, 35, 76–77
criollos, 81
crops. *See* farming
Cuesta, Arroyo de la, 45–46
Cutter, Donald C., 32, 47, 51, 61, 64

Dana, Charles Henry, 81–82
*Discovery of San Francisco Bay: The Portolá
  Expedition of 1769–1770, The,* (Costansó),
  16, 81
diseases, 44, 63–65
diversity, of population, 80–82

Dolores (mission). *See* San Francisco (mission)

Drake, Francis, 37

Duhaut-Cilly, Auguste, 34, 56, 63, 79

escolta (mission military escort), 82–83, 87, 89

Español (person of Spanish ancestry), 81, 84

explorers, 35

Fages, Pedro, 43

farming, 22, 44, 52–54

fathers. *See* Franciscan missionaries

Forbes, Jack D., 84

forts. *See* presidios

Franciscan missionaries

    clothing of, 75–77

    companionship and, 35

    dedication of, 79

    discipline of, 34, 67

    home life of, 77–78

    independence (of Mexico) and, 94–95

    isolation of, 78–79

    music and, 46

    personal qualities of, 36

    poverty of, 75–77

    success of, 44–45, 48

    time spent in California and, 34–35

    training of, 32–34

Franciscan nuns, 28

Franciscan order, 25–30, 76

Francis of Assisi, Saint, 25–26

Fray Juan Crespí, Missionary Explorer on the Pacific Coast 1769–1774, (Bolton), 35

friars. *See* Franciscan missionaries

Gálvez, Don José de, 10, 24, 35

Geiger, Maynard, 36, 88

gente de razón (non-Franciscan people of Spanish or Mexican descent in mission), 80–92

Gibson, Charles, 12

Hall, Trobridge, 46

Historical Memoirs (Palóu), 19

Hudson, Travis, 56, 59, 71, 73

Indian Life and Customs at Mission San Luis Rey: A Record of California Mission Life (Tac), 20, 40, 52, 76

Indian Life at the Old Missions (Webb), 73

Indians

    attacks of, on missions, 84

    described by early missionaries, 39–41

    diseases of Europeans and, 44, 63–65

    education of, 68–69

    enticements of missionaries for, 41–43

    health of, 63–65

    imprisonment of, by missionaries, 42

    languages of, 40, 46, 69

    mission life of, 49–66

    music as mission attraction for, 46

    pre-mission period lives of, 11, 38–39

    punishments for rule violations by, 65–66

    revolt against mission life of, 83

    Spanish citizenship and, 66

    work of, at missions, 51–59

Langsdorff, Georg H. von

    dedication of missionaries and, 79

    isolation of missions and, 78

    military and, 82–83

    mission ranching and, 55

    poverty of missionaries and, 75

    San José (mission) Indian attacks and, 84

La Pérouse, Jean-François de

    ceremonial items at missions and, 42–43

    Carmel (mission) and, 70

    conversion of Indians and, 47–48

    food preparation at missions and, 57–58

Franciscan missionaries and, 25
   Indian life at missions and, 50
   missionaries' lifestyles and, 77–78
La Purísima (mission), 17, 54, 83
Lasuén, Fermin Francisco de, 45
leather-jacket soldiers, 81, 85
Librado, Fernando, 56, 59, 71
Libro de Patentes (mission logbook), 72, 74
Life and Apostolic Labors of the Venerable Father Junípero Serra (Palóu), 26
Los Angeles (settlement), 90

matins (morning prayers), 34, 67
   see also mission ceremonies; rituals
mestizos (persons of mixed European and Mexican Indian ancestry), 81
Mexican War of Independence, 94
Mexico City, 10, 14
military, 80, 81–86
   see also presidios
missionaries. *See* Franciscan missionaries
Mission Dolores. *See* San Francisco (mission)
mission outposts, 55
mission period, 10, 11–13, 14
missions
   bells and, 20, 59, 67, 79
   building of, 23–24, 55–57
   business affairs of, 71–74
   ceremonies at, 20–21, 42, 46–47, 63, 67–68, 87
   children at, 59–62
   churches of, 24, 70–71, 91–92
   clothing at, 61, 75–77
   construction of, 23–24, 55–57
   decoration of, 70–71
   domestic animals at, 63
   education and, 62–63
   end of era of, 93–95
   family life at, 59–62
   farming and, 22, 44, 52–54

   festivals at, 63, 87
   food at, 44, 50, 51, 57–58
   goals of, 10, 11
   growth and prosperity of, 48
   hardships of life in, 30, 35
   home life at, 59–62
   Indian convert life at, 49–66
   Indian work at, 51–59
   invasions of, 85
   locations of, 14–17, 24
   medical care at, 44, 64
   music at, 59, 63, 69
   objectives of, 10, 11
   punishment of Indians at, 65–66
   ranching at, 55, 91
   reports and records of, 74
   richness (of ceremonial items) of, 42–43
   rituals of, 20–21, 42, 46–47, 63, 67–68
   rules of life at, 74
   schools of, 62–63
   secularization of, 94–95
   security and, 43–44
   self-sufficiency and, 21–22, 51–52
   sharing of property at, 52
   supplies for, 18, 44
   timekeeping at, 73
   tools and, 23
   War of Independence and, 94–95
   water supply at, 57
   work at, 51–59, 87
Mission Solano, 24
monasteries, 25–26
Monterey, 17
   see also Carmel (mission)
Monterey Bay, 14
mulattos (persons of mixed European and African ancestry), 81, 84
music, 59, 63, 69

Native Americans. *See* Indians
Native Californians. *See* Indians

neophytes. *See* Indians
New Spain, 10
novitiate, 27
    see also Franciscan order

ocean crossings, 31–32
Olbes, Ramon, 90–91

Paddison, Joshua, 42, 91, 94
Padrón (mission record), 71–72
Palóu, Francisco
    early mission decisions and, 14–15, 17
    Junípero Serra and, 25, 26
    motivation for mission work and, 30–31
    supplies for missions and, 18
Pico, Pio, 84
Pico, Santiago, 84
pirates, 85
Poor Clares, 28
pope, the, 10
    see also Alexander VI
presidios (forts), 11, 82, 85–86
priests. *See* Franciscan missionaries
pueblos (towns founded by Spanish), 89–92

quadrangle, 24

ranching, 54–55
religion. *See* Catholicism
Ripoll, Antonio, 23, 87
royalists, 81
Russians, 37

San Buenaventura (mission), 56, 59, 71, 83
San Carlos Borromeo de Carmelo. *See*
    Carmel (mission)
Sancho, Juan, 22
San Diego (mission), 10, 16–17, 82, 84
San Diego Bay, 14
San Francisco (mission), 70, 82, 84
San Francisco Bay, 14

San José (mission), 83, 84, 91
San José (settlement), 90, 91
San Juan Capistrano (mission), 85
San Luís Obispo (mission), 54
San Luis Rey (mission), 20, 45, 52, 63
Santa Barbara (mission), 46
    adobe making at, 59
    church at, 91–92
    church wall paintings at, 71
    Indian revolt at, 83
    isolation of, 79
    medical care at, 64–65
    presidio and, 82
    pueblo and, 91–92
    reliance of, on other missions, 54
    work contracts of, 88
Santa Clara (mission), 17, 83, 84
Santa Cruz (mission), 90, 91
Santa Inés (mission), 20, 83
Santa Maria, Vicente, 40–41
sea crossings, 31–32
Serra, Junípero
    biographical sketch of, 26
    Carmel (mission) and, 17, 21
    charisma of, 41
    childhood and youth of, 25
    companionship in missionary work and, 35
    food for converted Indians and, 43
    missionary work and, 29–31, 87
settlers, 90–91
    see also pueblos
siesta (nap), 78
Sisters of Saint Clare, 28
Spanish Tradition in America, The
    (Gibson), 12
Solá, Pablo Vicente, 87
Solano (mission), 45
soldados de cuera (Spanish leather-jacket
    soldiers), 81, 85
soldiers. *See* military; presidios
sundials, 73

Suñer, Francisco, 90

Tac, Pablo, 12–13, 20, 40, 52, 76
Tápis, Estévan, 58–59, 64, 65–66
temescals (sweat houses), 64
Tulare (tribe), 84

Vancouver, George, 70, 86, 91
Veracruz, 32, 78

viceroy, 10
Viscaíno, Sebastián, 37
voyages, 19, 31–32

War of Independence (Mexican), 94–95
Webb, Edith Buckland, 73
*World Transformed: Firsthand Accounts of
California Before the Gold Rush, A*
(Paddison), 42, 91, 94

Picture Credits

Cover photo: © North Wind Picture Archives
© Bettmann/CORBIS, 70
© Nancy Carter/North Wind Picture Archives, 1994, 26, 93
© CORBIS, 39, 60, 85
© Philip James Corwin/CORBIS, 17
© Richard Cummins/CORBIS, 34, 52
Jeff Di Matteo, 22, 54
© Michael Freeman/CORBIS, 46
© Historical Picture Archive/CORBIS, 33
© Honeychurch Antiques, Ltd./CORBIS, 27
© E.O. Hoppé/CORBIS, 74
© Hulton/Archive by Getty Images, 37, 65, 80
Chris Jouan, 24
William N. Patterson/Courtesy Mission San Juan Capistrano, 23, 43,
    50, 58, 68, 72, 78, 82, 89
North Wind Picture Archives, 15, 29, 31, 41, 44, 45, 49, 53, 57, 75,
    76, 86, 88
© Scala/Art Resource, NY, 28
© Paul Schermeister/CORBIS, 56, 62
© Stock Montage, Inc., 21

About the Author

Eileen Keremitsis holds an A.B. degree from the University of California at Berkeley and a Ph.D. in history from Columbia University. She writes a wide variety of nonfiction materials, but specializes in computers, travel, biography, and history. A native of California, she has also lived in Argentina, Bolivia, Brazil, Mexico, and France. Among the numerous awards she has received for academic and professional work is a Fulbright-Hays Research Fellowship for independent research in Rio de Janeiro, Brazil. She lives in San Francisco, California.